ANNE J. RICH
Quinnipiac College

STUDY GUIDE

MANAGERIAL ACCOUNTING

AN INTRODUCTION TO CONCEPTS, METHODS, AND USES

SIXTH EDITION

MICHAEL W. MAHER
University of California, Davis

CLYDE P. STICKNEY
Dartmouth College

ROMAN L. WEIL
University of Chicago

THE DRYDEN PRESS
Harcourt Brace College Publishers

Fort Worth   Philadelphia   San Diego   New York   Orlando   Austin   San Antonio
Toronto   Montreal   London   Sydney   Tokyo

Address for Editorial Correspondence
The Dryden Press, 301 Commerce Street, Suite 3700, Fort Worth, Texas 76102

Address for Orders
The Dryden Press, 6277 Sea Harbor Drive, Orlando, Florida 32887-6777
1-800-782-4479

ISBN: 0-03-018207-7

Printed in the United States of America

6 7 8 9 0 1 2 3 4 5   095   9 8 7 6 5 4 3 2 1

Contents

FOREWORD TO THE STUDENT

This study guide is designed to supplement Managerial Accounting: An Introduction to Concepts, Methods and Uses, Sixth Edition, by Michael W. Maher, Clyde P. Stickney, Roman I. Weil. A number of practice exercises are presented for each chapter, making it possible to use this study guide in conjunction with the text as a self-teaching package. Templates, which can be obtained from your instructor, are provided for selected problems to assist you.

Organization of the book: This study guide contains seventeen chapters corresponding to those found in the book.

Organization of the chapters: Each chapter in this study guide is generally structured according to the following pattern of organization:

1. An introduction to the chapter.
2. Learning objectives.
3. Textbook exhibits. Pay close attention to what the exhibits are communicating.
4. A review of key concepts. This section serves as an outline of the chapter to help you review all of the essential information presented in the textbook chapter.
5. Key terms. Be sure you have a good understanding of these basic terms.
6. Self-test. Accounting concepts are best understood when they are applied to specific situations. This section includes short, simple problems that will help you complete the exercises and problems in the text.
7. Solutions to the study guide exercises. The answers give you immediate feedback and direct your attention to areas that need review.

8. A study plan. The plan points to particular exhibits in the text that should be reviewed and identifies approaches to solving some of the textbook problems. This section refers you to the problems for which templates are available from your instructor. To make use of these templates, students will need access to a spreadsheet program compatible with LOTUS 1-2-3 ® or Microsoft EXCEL ®. This disk, provided to you by your instructor, contains templates for the following textbook problems:

2-26	7-26	13-31
2-31	8-24	13-34
3-24	8-31	14-19
3-33	8-38	14-24
4-23	9-19	14-30
4-24	9-21	15-32
4-25	9-23	15-34
4-36	9-29	15-35
5-34	10-25	15-38
5-38	10-32	16-16
5-40	10-37	16-17
6-18	10-39	16-19
6-28	11-29	16-21
6-29	11-37	17-14
7-17	11-38	17-16
7-18	11-46	17-18
7-24	13-21	17-34
	13-22	

Chapter 1

Managerial Uses of Accounting Information

This first chapter presents an overview of the use of management accounting information and provides a comparison of managerial and financial accounting. Accounting provides information for managerial decision making, planning, managerial control and internal performance evaluation, as well as financial reporting for external performance evaluation by shareholders and creditors. Key financial players in the organization are identified. You will learn about the managerial accountant's professional environment and ethical responsibilities. Activity-based management, the value chain, as well as just-in-time and lean production, quality management and benchmarking concepts are introduced. The importance of effective communication between accountants and users of managerial accounting information is stressed. This chapter begins the study of managerial accounting by introducing fundamental relationships and uses of managerial accounting. Your overall objective in this chapter is to understand the role that managerial accounting information plays in communicating for decision making, planning, control, and performance evaluation.

LEARNING OBJECTIVES

LO1   Distinguish between managerial and financial accounting

LO2   Understand the use of accounting information for decision making, planning, control, and performance evaluation.

LO3   Identify the key financial players in the organization

LO4   Understand managerial accountants' professional environment and ethical responsibilities.

LO5   Explain the benefits of activity-based management and application of the value chain.

LO6   Describe how managerial accounting supports the new production environment.

LO7   Understand the importance of effective communication between accountants and users of managerial accounting information.

LO8   Understand the ethical standards that comprise the Institute of Management Accountants' Code of Ethics (Appendix 1.1 in text).

TEXTBOOK EXHIBITS

Exhibit 1-1 illustrates the relationship among the three principal uses of accounting information: decision making, planning and control, and performance evaluation. Note the decision making process begins with identifying a problem or objective, then accounting and other information is gathered, a decision is made, and an outcome is specified. During the period, actual results are collected and summarized in a format that can be compared to the original expectations. A performance report measures the differences between what was expected and the actual results obtained.

Exhibit 1-2 illustrates the organization of the E. I. du Pont de Nemours and Company corporation. Financial managers at the corporate level are shown in the shaded boxes. The top financial person is often called the vice-president of finance. The controller, who is in charge of cost and managerial accounting, reports to the finance vice-president.

Exhibit 1-3 provides an overview of the value chain. Note that the six activities include research and development, design, production, marketing, distribution, and customer service. Activities that add value increase the usefulness of the products or services of an organization.

Exhibit 1-4 shows how users, after identifying their information needs, request data from accountants. The analysis of costs and benefits requires considerable communication and cooperation between users and accountants.

REVIEW OF KEY CONCEPTS

LO1   Users of financial information are traditionally split into two groups:

    A. **Financial accounting** refers to the generation of general-purpose reports for use by persons outside the organization. These persons are called external users. External users include groups with very diverse motivations and interests. Stockholders, bondholders, other creditors, and government agencies all have an interest in the financial information provided by the company.

    B. **Managerial accounting** provides information to individuals inside the organization. Managers of all kinds of organizations (manufacturing, retail, service, and nonprofit) need information to make decisions. Often general-purpose financial statements do not provide sufficient detail or the right format for managerial decisions. Managerial accounting focuses on information which will aid managers in making decisions, and in planning and controlling business operations.

LO2   Managerial accounting aids managers in (1) managerial-decision making and planning, (2) managerial control and internal performance evaluation, and (3) financial reporting for external performance evaluation by shareholders and creditors.

    A. **Managerial-decision making and planning** includes identifying problems, objectives or goals, as well as identifying possible alternatives.

    B. The next step requires gathering accounting and other information about the expected outcomes for the alternative actions.

    C. Managers then make a decision.

    D. Managers must specify the outcome expected as a result of their decision.

    E. During the period, actual results for the project are summarized and presented in a report that compares actual results to the expected outcome. Recording data is part of the **control** system.

F.   During the performance evaluation stage, reports are generated for both **internal performance evaluation** and control as well as for **external performance evaluation** purposes.

Test Your Understanding

Question: When a problem is identified, why should several alternative actions also be identified?

Answer: Managers have a responsibility to consider many possible alternative courses of actions in order to assess the costs and benefits of each one. If managers simply identify one possible solution, other strategies, which may be more effective, may never be considered.

LO3   The key financial players in organization are the following persons:

A.   The **Financial vice-president** is usually the senior vice-president in the company. The financial vice-president is in charge of the entire accounting and finance function.

B.   The **Controller** is in charge of cost and managerial accounting functions. The controller is involved in planning, decision making, designing information systems, designing incentive systems, and helping managers make operating decisions.

C.   The **Treasurer** is in charge of raising cash for operations and managing cash and near-cash assets. The treasurer normally handles relations with banks and other lenders and manages public issues of the company's shares or debt.

D.   The **cost accountants** record and analyze costs. They work in teams with people from other functions, such as marketing and engineering.

E.   The **internal auditors** provide a variety of auditing and consulting services. Operational auditors focus on operating efficiencies while financial auditors concentrate on the accuracy of financial information for the external financial statements.

LO4   The professional environment includes:

A. Following **generally accepted accounting principles (GAAP)** whenever financial reports are prepared for external users.

B. Being familiar with the policies and pronouncements of the **Institute of Management Accountants (IMA)**. The IMA is a professional organization composed of individuals who work as management accountants.

C. Recognizing the professional designation, the **Certified Management Accountant (CMA)** as a designation reflecting educational achievement and professional competence in management accounting.

D. Understanding that the *Internal Revenue Code* (tax legislation passed by the U.S. Congress) influences management decisions.

E. Being familiar with the regulations of the **Cost Accounting Standards Board (CASB)**, a federal organization responsible for setting accounting standards for government contracts with defense contractors.

F. In Canada, recognizing organizations that provide designations similar to the designations in the U.S. These are the **Chartered Accountant (CA)** and the **Certified General Accountant (CGA)**, which are similar to the CPA designation in the U.S. and the **Certified Management Accountant (CMA)** which is similar to the CMA designation in the U.S.

LO4   The professional environment includes an awareness of ethical issues.

A. Companies hold managers accountable for achieving financial performance targets. As a result, organizations exert great pressure on managers. This pressure could result in a manager being tempted to manipulate accounting numbers to make them look better than actual results. Understanding the warning signs leading to **fraudulent reporting** will help managers protect themselves and set the proper ethical tone in the workplace.

B. The Institute of Management Accountant has a **code of conduct** called *"Standards of Ethical Conduct for Management Accountants."* The IMA code mandates that management accountants have a responsibility to maintain the highest levels of ethical conduct. Steps to resolve ethical conflicts are specified in the code.

LO5 **Activity-based management (ABM)** studies activities that cause costs in organizations.

A. Under activity-based management (ABM) companies are able to reduce costs by understanding what activities cause costs. Managers develop plans to reduce non-value-added activities and to improve efficiency of value-added activities.

B. **Value-added activities** are activities that increase the product's service to the customer. Alternatively, nonvalue-added activities add to costs and could be eliminated without impairing the product's value. Idle time is an example of a nonvalue-added activity.

C. **The value chain** describes the linked set of activities that increase the usefulness, or value, of the products and services of an organization. All activities are evaluated with reference to how that activity contributes to the final product's service, quality, and cost. The value chain includes the following six functions:
   1. research and development
   2. design
   3. production
   4. marketing
   5. distribution
   6. customer service

D. **Strategic cost analysis** is a process where managers can identify strategic advantages in the marketplace by analyzing the value chain and information about the costs of activities.

E. Managers should consider **global strategies** as a way of gaining cost advantages.

LO6   Managerial accounting in the new production environment requires managers to be aware of new technologies and new management philosophies. These include just-in-time and lean production, quality management, theory of constraints, as well as benchmarking and continuous improvement.

    A. **Just-in-time production (JIT)** is part of a "lean production" philosophy that eliminates inventory between production departments. Inventory carrying costs are reduced and less time is spent accounting for inventory. **Lean production** requires the flexibility to change quickly from one product to another.

    B. **Total quality management (TQM)** refers to excelling in all dimensions. In TQM, the focus is on satisfying the customer. Performance measures to support a TQM system would include financial and nonfinancial information, such as product reliability, service delivery, and customer satisfaction.

    C. **The theory of constraints (TOC)** views the business as a linked sequence of processes that transform inputs into salable outputs. To improve the process, the weakest link in the chain is identified and resources are applied to strengthen that part of the chain.

    D. **Benchmarking** is the process of measuring one's own products, services, and activities against the best level of performance.

    E. **Continuous improvement** reflects managers desires to seek ongoing improvement.

LO7   Communication between accountants and users of managerial accounting information is critical to the success of a company. Accountants and managers must work together to assess the **costs and benefits** of information.

Test Your Understanding

Question: Would managers or accountants be less concerned about the costs of generating information? Who is in a better position to assess the benefits?

Answer: Managers would most likely not consider the cost of information. Managers usually request more information than they need to make a decision. On the other hand, managers may benefit from information in a special format. Thus, accountants and managers must work together to provide relevant information on a timely basis to managers who must make decisions.

LO8   The **Institute of Management Accountants'** *Standards of Ethical Conduct for Management Accountants* guides the behavior of management accountants. Members of the IMA have an obligation to maintain high standards of ethical conduct.

    A.   They must maintain their competency in the field by ongoing development of their knowledge and skills.

    B.   They have a responsibility to maintain confidentiality.

    C.   They must maintain personal integrity and avoid conflicts of interest.

    D.   They must be objective and communicate information fairly and objectively.

    E.   They must follow guidelines in the code concerning resolution of ethical conflict. To resolve an ethical conflict, a management accountant should:
       1.   Begin with following the established policies of the organization to resolve the problem.
       2.   If still unresolved, discuss the problem with the immediate supervisor except when it appears that the supervisor is involved.
       3.   If still unresolved, contact with levels above the immediate supervisor.
       4.   Clarify relevant concepts by confidential discussion with an objective advisor to obtain an understanding of the possible courses of action.
       5.   If the ethical conflict still exists, the management accountant may have no other alternative than to resign from the organization and to submit an informative memorandum to an appropriate representative of the organization.

KEY TERMS

LO1 Distinguish between managerial and financial accounting.

Managerial accounting	Reporting designed to enhance the ability of management to do its job of decision making, planning, and control.
Financial accounting	The accounting for assets, liabilities, equities, revenues and expenses of a business.

LO3 Identify the key financial players in the organization.

Financial vice-president	The person who is in charge of the entire accounting and finance function.
Controller	The person who is in charge of cost and managerial accounting; also involved in planning, decision making, designing information systems, designing incentive systems, helping managers make operating decisions, and a variety of other activities.
Treasurer	The person who is in charge of raising cash for operations and managing cash and near-cash assets.
Cost accountant	The internal accountant who records and analyzes costs and works on teams with other organization members for analysis and decision making.
Internal audit	An audit conducted by employees inside the organization to test whether internal control procedures are working and whether the company's policies are being carried out..

LO4 Understand managerial accountants' professional environment and ethical responsibilities.

Generally accepted accounting principles (GAAP)	As defined by the Financial Accounting Standards Board, the conventions, rules, and procedures necessary to define accepted accounting practice for external reporting at a particular time.
Institute of Management Accountants (IMA)	Organization of management accountants that oversees administration of the CMA examination.
Certified Management Accountant (CMA)	Designation awarded by the Institute of Management Accountants to those who pass a set of examinations and meet certain experience and continuing education requirements.
Certified Public Accountant (CPA)	An accountant who has satisfied the statutory and administrative requirements of his or her jurisdiction to be registered or licensed as a public accountant.
Cost Accounting Standards Board (CASB)	A board authorized by the U.S. Congress to promulgate standards designed to achieve uniformity and consistency in the cost accounting principles followed by defense contractors and subcontractors.

LO5 Explain the benefits of activity-based management and application of the value chain.

Activity-based management (ABM)	The analysis and management of the activities Focuses management's attention to enhance those activities that add value to the customer and eliminate those that do not add value. Also called **activity management**.

Value chain   The business functions associated with increasing the usefulness, or value, of the products or services of an organization (value-added activities).

Value-added activity   Activity that increases the product's services to the customer.

Nonvalue-added activity   Any activity that when eliminated reduces costs without reducing the product's service potential to the customer.

LO6 Describe how managerial accounting supports the new production environment.

Just-in-time (JIT)   System of managing inventory in which a firm purchases or manufacturers each component just before it is used.

Total quality management (TQM) Concept by which an organization is managed to excel on all dimensions, and quality is ultimately defined by the customer.

Theory of constraints (TOC)   A system of improving operations by identifying and eliminating constraints within a process.

Benchmarking   The continuous process of measuring one's own products, services, and activities against the best level of performance.

LO7 Understand the importance of effective communication between accountants and users of managerial accounting information.

Cost-benefit criterion

Some measure of costs compared to some measure of benefits for a proposed undertaking. If the costs exceed the benefits, then the analyst judges the undertaking not worthwhile.

SELF-TEST

LO1 1. COMPARISON OF FINANCIAL AND MANAGERIAL ACCOUNTING

For each of the following statements, indicate whether the function is more closely associated with financial or managerial accounting:

_____a. Reports are directed to external users
_____b. Need not comply with GAAP
_____c. Uses historic data in evaluating performance of the firm
_____d. Internal cost/benefit criterion dictates how much information is needed
_____e. Presents more detailed information about product lines, costs, revenues and profits

LO2 2. BUSINESS DECISION MAKING

Upon graduating from college, B.J. Smith and N.E. Jones decided they would open their own computer consulting business. They are trying to decide on using their home as an office or renting space in a commercial building. Identify the costs and benefits of each alternative.

a. Using the home as an office:

1 Costs:

2. Benefits:

b. Renting space in a commercial building:

    1 Costs:

    2. Benefits:

LO8   3.   RESOLVING AN ETHICAL DILEMMA

Jennifer Green is the controller for a division of a large company. The division's manager requests Ms. Green approve travel for a trip that she believes will have no business purpose. Jennifer is a member of the Institute of Management Accountants. What steps are required for Jennifer Green to follow in resolving this dilemma?

SOLUTIONS

1. COMPARISON OF FINANCIAL AND MANAGERIAL ACCOUNTING
    a. Financial accounting
    b. Financial accounting
    c. Financial accounting
    d. Managerial accounting
    e. Managerial accounting

2. BUSINESS DECISION MAKING

    a. Using the home as an office:
        Financial costs include extra electricity and heat, extra telephone lines and office equipment. Nonfinacial costs include the interruptions caused by family members.
        Benefits include the convenience of home.

    b. Using a commercial building:
        Financial costs include legal fees, rent, electricity and heat, and office equipment. Nonfinancial costs include the time to get to the office. Benefits include more professional atmosphere.

3. RESOLVING AN ETHICAL DILEMMA

    Jennifer Green must follow the guidelines established by the Institute of Management Accounting in the Standards of Ethical Conduct for Management Accountants. Thus, she must first follow established policies of the organization to resolve the problem. Perhaps there is an ombudsman to assist her. If still unresolved, she should discuss the problem with her immediate superior unless it is the supervisor who is making this request. If still unresolved, she should communicate with individuals at a level above the immediate supervisor. She has a responsibility to clarify relevant concepts by confidential discussion with an objective advisor to obtain an understanding of the possible courses of action. If she still feels that she cannot approve the travel, and believes an ethical conflict still exists, Jennifer Green may have no other alternative than to resign from the organization and to submit an informative memorandum to an appropriate representative of the organization. In no case should she reveal the problem to people outside the organization, unless legally obligated to do so.

STUDY PLAN

At the end of each chapter, you will be presented with a study plan. Your review of each chapter should begin by looking at each of the key exhibits to gain an overview of the chapter. Next, look at the key terms. At this point you should be able to provide a definition for each of the key terms. If a term is not clear to you, you should refer to the text.

Chapter 2

◆

Cost Concepts for Managerial Decision Making

This chapter introduces what accounting means by the term cost. You will learn what costs are required to make a product and how to distinguish between fixed and variable costs. The chapter highlights the role differential cost analysis for decision making and defines gross margin, contribution margin, and profit margin. Income statements are presented in a traditional format for stockholders and in a different format for use in managerial decisions. This alternative format is the contribution approach.

LEARNING OBJECTIVES

LO1 Master the concept of cost.
LO2 Distinguish between direct and indirect costs.
LO3 Distinguish between manufacturing and nonmanufacturing costs.
LO4 Understand the nature of common, or indirect costs.
LO5 Compare, contrast, and compute gross margin, contribution margin, and profit margin.
LO6 Compare and contrast an income statement prepared for managerial use and one prepared for external reporting.

LO7   Understand the use of the value chain concept in preparing income statements for managerial use.

TEXTBOOK EXHIBITS

Exhibit 2.1 shows the cost of producing a good. It identifies the prime costs as direct materials and direct labor. Factory overhead, which consists of rent, utilities, indirect materials, indirect labor, and other costs, attach to the product. Nonmanufacturing costs are not considered part of the cost of producing a good.

Exhibit 2.2 shows what makes up a product's costs. The variable manufacturing costs include direct materials, direct labor, and variable manufacturing overhead. When fixed manufacturing costs are assigned to the product, the full-absorption cost for inventory purposes is determined. The variable costs of the product include not only the manufacturing variable costs, but also the variable marketing and administrative costs. The full cost of the product includes all the variable costs and all the fixed costs across all functions: manufacturing, marketing, and administrative.

Exhibit 2.3 illustrates the components of the gross margin. Gross margin is sales less the full absorption cost and is used for external financial reporting.

Exhibit 2.4 illustrates the components of the contribution margin. Contribution margin is sales less all the variable costs of producing, selling and administering.

Exhibit 2.5 presents an income statement format appropriate for external reporting. The gross margin is calculated.

Exhibit 2.6 presents an income statement format appropriate for internal reporting. The contribution margin is calculated.

Exhibit 2.7 provides an example of an income statement for managerial decision making using value chain concepts.

REVIEW OF KEY CONCEPTS

LO1   Managers need information concerning the costs of operating an organization.

   A. **Costs** are sacrifices of resources.

   B. In economics, and in accounting, the **opportunity cost** concept assists us in making rational decisions. The opportunity cost is defined as the cost of using an asset for an alternative use other than the best one for it. It is the cost a company must bear if it chooses not to make the best use of its resources. Managers sometimes choose to bear this cost in current periods in order to achieve their long-run strategic goals.

C. Cost, or sacrifices, are important managerial terms. In managerial accounting, we are concerned with **costs,** and not with **expenses.** In financial accounting, expenses (or expired assets) are measured in order to prepare financial statements consistent with generally accepted accounting principles (GAAP) and assigned to a particular accounting period.

LO2 Distinction between direct and indirect costs

A. A useful classification of costs includes direct and indirect costs. **Direct** costs are related to a cost object and need no special allocation. A cost object is any item for which the manager wishes to measure cost.

B. **Indirect** costs, on the other hand, must be allocated by a formula in order to be associated with a cost object. It is possible for an item to be considered direct to one cost object and indirect to another. For example, rent is direct to a sales office but is indirect to the products sold from that office. Thus, it is important to first identify the cost object and then to classify the cost.

C. **Common costs** are indirect costs shared by two or more cost objects. Usually a cost is indirect because it is considered a common cost that must be allocated to two or more cost objects. For example, the salary of a supervisor who is responsible for two departments is first allocated to each department because it is a common cost and then each product produced within each department is made to absorb some of the indirect salary allocated to the department.

D. One of the most useful classifications for managerial decision making is the distinction between fixed and variable costs. **Variable costs** increase in total as some activity increases. A **fixed cost** remains constant over a wide range of activity.

LO3 Distinction between manufacturing and nonmanufacturing costs

A. The type of organization and the nature of its activities affect costs. Manufacturing, for example, involves the transformation of materials into finished goods. It is the most complex organization in terms of costs.

B. The cost of a manufactured unit includes its **direct materials, direct labor,** and **manufacturing overhead.** The term **prime costs** refers to the essential inputs, direct materials, and direct labor. The term **conversion costs** refers to the elements necessary to convert the materials into its final form, namely, direct labor and manufacturing overhead.

C. Following GAAP, costs attach to assets first. In computing the costs of goods sold, companies must consider the impact of beginning and ending inventory. Manufacturing costs attach to the asset called inventory and are referred to as **product costs.** When the inventory is sold, the expense for the period is referred to as the cost of goods sold. The cost of goods sold is a **period cost.**

D. Nonmanufacturing costs include marketing costs and general administrative costs. The income statement will show these costs separate from the product costs. Marketing and administrative costs are also period costs.

E. Service organizations do not have inventory of goods for sale. Often the service organization's product is less tangible and difficult to measure. Many of the costs associated with service organizations are indirect.

LO4   Understand the nature of common, or indirect costs.

A. Many costs are common to different products or services.

B. Managers use allocated costs to develop unit cost information about their products and services. Unit cost information is useful in pricing and bidding.

C. Some contracts require companies to allocate common costs to determine the amount to be paid.

D. Companies allocate costs to operating units to motivate certain behaviors.

LO5   Gross Margin, Contribution Margin, and Profit Margin

A. The components of a product cost includes its variable manufacturing costs, fixed manufacturing costs, variable marketing and administrative costs, and the fixed marketing and administrative costs.

B. The **unit profit margin** is calculated by subtracting the full cost per unit of making and selling the product from the unit selling price.

C. The **full absorption cost** is the sum of the manufacturing costs (direct materials, direct labor, variable and fixed manufacturing overhead).

D. The **full cost** of a product or service includes not only the full absorption cost (the manufacturing costs), but also the selling and administrative costs.

E. The difference between the unit selling price and the unit full absorption cost is the **unit gross margin**.

F. The difference between the sales revenue and the variable manufacturing, selling, and administrative costs is called the **contribution margin**.

G. The difference between the sales revenue and the full cost of the product is the **profit margin**.

Test Your Understanding

Question: Assume a company has the following manufacturing costs;

Direct materials per unit	$10
Direct labor per unit	15
Variable overhead per unit	5
Fixed overhead per unit	8

What is the full absorption cost per unit?

Answer: $38 because the full absorption cost includes all of the above costs.

LO6   Compare and contrast income statements prepared for managerial use and those prepared for external reporting.

A. The income statement for external reporting follows a traditional format (see Exhibit 2.5) The first section reports sales less cost of goods sold. The cost of goods sold includes all the manufacturing costs (direct materials, direct labor, variable manufacturing overhead, and fixed manufacturing overhead).

B. The income statement for internal reporting follows a contribution format (see Exhibit 2.6). The first section reports the sales less the variable costs. The variable costs include the variable cost of goods sold (direct materials, direct labor, and variable manufacturing overhead) as well as the variable marketing and administrative expenses. All of the fixed costs, manufacturing and nonmnaufacturing, are deducted after the contribution margin.

LO7   The use of the value chain concepts in preparing income statements for managerial use.

    A. Companies should consider developing financial statements that classify costs into value-added or nonvalue-added categories.

    B. By classifying activities as value-added or nonvalue-added, managers are better able to focus on which activities to reduce or eliminate and therefore reduce costs.

    C. Exhibit 2.7 provides an example of an income statement for managerial decision making using value chain concepts.

KEY TERMS

LO1 The concept of cost

Opportunity cost	The cost of using an asset for an alternative use other than the best one for it.

LO2 Distinguish between direct and indirect costs

Direct costs	The costs of direct materials and direct labor incurred in producing a product.
Indirect costs	The costs of production not easily associated with the production of specific goods and services, also called overhead.
Cost object	Any item for which to measure cost - for example, a facility, department, or product.

LO3 Distinguish between manufacturing and nonmanufacturing costs

Manufacturing costs	The costs of producing goods, including direct materials, direct labor, and manufacturing overhead.
Nonmanufacturing costs	All costs incurred other than those to produce goods, including marketing, administrative, merchandise, and research and development costs.
Direct materials	Materials applied and assigned directly to a product.
Indirect materials	Materials not easily associated with a specific unit of product, such as supplies.
Direct labor	Cost of labor applied and assigned directly to a product.
Indirect labor	Labor not easily associated with a particular unit of product, such as a supervisor's salary.
Manufacturing overhead	General manufacturing costs incurred in providing a capacity to carry on productive activities not directly associated with identifiable units of product.
Prime cost	Sum of direct materials and direct labor.
Conversion costs	The costs to convert raw materials to finished products; includes direct labor and manufacturing.
Merchandise costs	Costs incurred to acquire merchandise for resale.
Marketing costs	Costs incurred to sell a product-- for example, commissions and advertising.

Administrative costs	Costs incurred for operating the firm as a whole -- the salary of the managerial accountant, for example.
Research and development costs	All costs of developing new products and services.
Product costs	Any manufacturing cost that can be inventoried. Includes direct materials, direct labor, and manufacturing overhead.
Period costs	Expenditures, usually based on the passage of time, charged to operations of the accounting period. Includes nonmanufacturing costs, such as marketing and administrative.
Full absorption costing	The method of costing that assigns all types of manufacturing costs to units produced, required by GAAP.
Variable costing	Method of allocating costs that assigns only variable manufacturing costs to products and treats fixed manufacturing costs as period expenses.
Variable costs	Costs that change as activity levels change.
Fixed costs	Costs that do not vary with volume of activity in the short run.

LO4 Understand the nature of common, or indirect costs.

Common costs	Costs resulting from the use of raw materials, a facility, or a service that benefits several products or departments.

LO5 Compare, contrast, and compute gross margin, contribution margin, and profit margin.

Gross margin	Sales minus full absorption cost (the manufacturing costs).
Contribution margin	Sales minus all variable expenses.
Profit margin	Sales minus the full cost of the product (all manufacturing, marketing and administrative costs).

SELF-TEST

LO1   1.   IDENTIFICATION OF COST TERMS

Robert Baker, a marketing major, has to decide which course to enroll in during the summer semester. He noted that a computer course he wanted to take was offered at a cost of $600 plus fees for computer time charges at the rate of $25 per hour. His other choice is a management course. The tuition for the management course is $850 because of a field trip requirement. In addition to selecting a course, Robert needs a place to stay during the summer. While he already paid $1,000 for a dormitory room, Robert decided he could no longer live with his roommate. There are two rooms available: a private residence that would cost him $1,400 and a semi-private room that would cost $1,100. Robert could sublet his dormitory but feels he should keep it empty in case he changes his mind and returns to campus.

REQUIRED: Identify the following:

a.   An opportunity cost

b.   A fixed cost

c.   A variable cost

LO6   2.   PREPARING INCOME STATEMENTS

The Ambose Company makes a single product. Assume the following facts:

Units produced during the year	2,000	units
Units sold during the year	2,000	units
Selling price per unit	$15.00	per unit
Variable manufacturing costs per unit:		
Direct materials	$2.00	per unit
Direct labor	$1.50	per unit
Variable manufacturing overhead	$1.00	per unit
Fixed manufacturing costs	$5,000	per year
Marketing and administrative:		
Fixed costs	$3,000	per year
Variable costs	$3.00	per unit

REQUIRED:

a.   Prepare an income statement for external reporting showing the gross margin.

b. Prepare an income statement for internal reporting showing the contribution margin.

c. Which income statement is more useful to making managerial decisions? Why?

LO7.   3.   VALUE-CHAIN CONCEPTS

Using the Ambrose Company information in Exercise 2, how could the company use the value-chain concepts to improve the report to managers?

SOLUTIONS

1. IDENTIFICATION OF COST TERMS:

   a. The foregone rent from subletting his dormitory is an example of an opportunity cost.
   b. His monthly rent is a fixed cost.
   c. The hourly charge for computer time is a variable cost.

2. PREPARING INCOME STATEMENTS:

   a.
Sales		$30,000
Less cost of goods sold:		
Variable manufacturing	$9,000	
Fixed manufacturing	5,000	14,000
Gross Margin		16,000
Less marketing and administrative costs:		
Variable mkg. & adm.	$6,000	
Fixed mkg. & adm.	3,000	9,000
Operating Profit		$7,000

   b.
Sales		$30,000
Less variable costs:		
Cost of goods sold	$9,000	
Mkg. & adm.	6,000	15,000
Contribution Margin		15,000
Less fixed costs:		
Manufacturing	5,000	
Mkg & adm.	3,000	8,000
Operating profit		$7,000

   c. The contribution margin format is more useful to managers because it provides the contribution margin and clearly separates costs into its fixed and variable components.

3. VALUE-CHAIN CONCEPTS
   Managers should classify all activities as value-added or nonvalue-added. Then, using a format similar to Exhibit 2.7 in the text, managers could focus their attention on reducing the nonvalue-added costs in the product.

STUDY PLAN

1. Review the learning objectives, exhibits, and key terms for this chapter.

2. Look at Problem 2.1 for Self Study in the text. Classify each of the items as variable or fixed, and direct or indirect to the product. Then classify each of the items by function (manufacturing, marketing, or administrative).

	Direct/Indirect	Fixed/Variable	Function
(a) Sandpaper, nails, varnish	_____	_____	_____
(b) Leather	_____	_____	_____
(c) Factory rent	_____	_____	_____
(d) Labor - cutting	_____	_____	_____
(e) Supervisor's salary	_____	_____	_____
(f) Maintenance and depreciation - fixed	_____	_____	_____
(g) Utilities-factory - fixed	_____	_____	_____
(h) Sven's salary	_____	_____	_____
(i) Labor - assembling	_____	_____	_____
(j) Sales commission	_____	_____	_____
(k) Shipping cost	_____	_____	_____
(l) Adm. manager's salary	_____	_____	_____
(m) Office supplies	_____	_____	_____
(n) Adm. secretary's salary	_____	_____	_____
(o) Wood	_____	_____	_____
(p) Advertising	_____	_____	_____

Answer:

		Direct/ Indirect	Fixed/ Variable	Function
(a)	Sandpaper, nails, varnish	Indirect	Variable	Manufacturing
(b)	Leather	Direct	Variable	Manufacturing
(c)	Factory rent	Indirect	Fixed	Manufacturing
(d)	Labor - cutting	Direct	Variable	Manufacturing
(e)	Supervisor's salary	Indirect	Fixed	Manufacturing
(f)	Maintenance and depreciation - fixed	Indirect	Fixed	Manufacturing
(g)	Utilities -factory - fixed	Indirect	Fixed	Manufacturing
(h)	Sven's salary	Indirect	Fixed	Administrative
(i)	Labor - assembling	Direct	Variable	Manufacturing
(j)	Sales commission	Indirect	Variable	Marketing
(k)	Shipping cost	Indirect	Variable	Marketing
(l)	Adm. manager's salary	Indirect	Fixed	Administrative
(m)	Office supplies	Indirect	Variable	Administrative
(n)	Adm. secretary's salary	Indirect	Fixed	Administrative
(o)	Wood	Indirect	Fixed	Manufacturing
(p)	Advertising	Indirect	Fixed	Marketing

Note: Many costs would be classified differently under different situations. For example, utilities and maintenance may behave as a variable cost in some companies. Similarly, a secretary's salary could vary based on the number of hours worked each week.

3. Look again at Problem 2.1 for Self Study. in the text. What is Klog's capacity? In Self Study Problem 2.1 the capacity is 100,000 units. Suppose the company wished to increase sales by 40,000 units. What additional information would managers need? Answer: In order to increase sales, which is currently at 70,000 units, by an additional 40,000 units, the company may incur additional capacity costs, like rent for additional space or equipment. In addition, managers would have to estimate if the variable costs of producing would change as a result of the new level of production. Cost information is reliable only for a given range of volume. In Self-Study Problem 2.1 the information is useful only for a volume up to 100,000 units.

4. Review Exhibits 2.3 and 2.4 in the text. You should be able to compute gross margin, contribution margin, and profit margin.

5. Use the template that accompanies the text to solve Problem 2-26. Use Exhibits 2.2 and 2.3 to help you remember how to compute the gross margin, contribution margin, and gross profit.

6. Use the template that accompanies the text to solve Problem 2-31. It will assist you in setting up the problem. Be careful in how you utilize the common fixed costs. Remember, these are allocated costs and are common to many products.

Chapter 3

◆

Estimating Cost Behavior

This chapter presents the nature of fixed and variable costs. The effects of learning on costs is demonstrated. Graphs of semivariable and semifixed costs are shown. The chapter describes how analysts estimate cost behavior using engineering methods and account analysis. Cost curves are visually created. Regression results are explained and used in estimating the effects of alternative cost drivers. The strengths and weaknesses of alternative cost estimation methods are discussed.

LEARNING OBJECTIVES

LO1   Distinguish between variable costs and fixed costs, and between short run and long run, and define the relevant range.

LO2   Identify capacity costs, committed costs, and discretionary costs.

LO3   Understand the nature of various cost behavior patterns.

LO4   Describe how managers use cost behavior patterns.

LO5   Understand how analysts estimate cost behavior using engineering methods and account analysis.

LO6   Use historical cost data to estimate cost.

LO7   Explain the costs, benefits, and weaknesses of various cost estimation methods.

LO8   Know how learning curves are derived (Appendix 3.1 in the text).

LO9   Interpret the results of regression analyses (Appendix 3.2 in the text).

TEXTBOOK EXHIBITS

Exhibit 3.1 provides a comparison of how costs behave in the short run and the long run. The concept of relevant range is highlighted.

Exhibits 3.2 through **3.4** show when projected volume is outside the relevant range management must take care to consider any changes in the fixed costs.

Exhibit 3.5 provides examples of curvilinear variable cost behavior.

Exhibit 3.6 shows the impact of learning curves on time and cost behavior.

Exhibit 3.7 graphs semivariable and semifixed cost behaviors.

Exhibit 3.8 demonstrates the use of account analysis.

Exhibit 3.9 provides the information for estimating costs.

Exhibit 3.10 demonstrates the use of regression analysis.

Exhibit 3.11 compares the regression estimate to possible nonlinear results.

Exhibit 3.12 summarizes the strengths and weaknesses of cost estimation methods.

REVIEW OF KEY CONCEPTS

LO1   Distinguish between variable costs and fixed costs, and between short run and long run, and define the relevant range.

    A.   Conceptually, all costs are classified as fixed or variable. **Variable costs,** also known as **engineered costs,** are costs that change as the level of activity changes (although they are constant per unit). **Fixed costs** do not change as activity level changes (but unit costs change).

    B.   Over long time spans no costs are fixed because all costs can be eliminated. The concept of short run and long run are important in managerial accounting. **The short run** is a time period long enough to allow management to change the level of production or other activity with the constraints of current total productive capacity. In the short run, costs that vary with activity level are variable costs. Costs that do not vary in the short run are fixed costs.

    C.   Management can change total productive capacity only in the **long run.**

    D.   The accounting concepts of fixed and variable costs are short-run concepts.

    E.   The definition of fixed cost assumes a short-run orientation and a specified **relevant range.** Total production capacity can only be changed in the long run. The relevant range is also an important concept in estimating cost behavior. The relevant range is the level of activity likely to be undertaken with the existing plant.

LO2   Identify capacity costs, committed costs, and discretionary costs.

A.   Costs classified as fixed fall into two categories: capacity and discretionary.

B.   **Capacity costs** provide a firm with the facilities to produce or to sell or both. Capacity costs are also called **committed costs**.

C.   **Discretionary costs** are not necessary in the short run to operate a business, but are essential for achieving long-term goals. An example of a discretionary cost is research cost.

LO3   Understand the nature of various cost behavior patterns.

A.   Perfectly straight fixed and variable cost behavior patterns are not always found in practice.

B.   **Curvilinear costs** vary with volume but not proportionally. Often this occurs as a result of learning acquired from experience in making the product.

C.   There is often systematic learning from experience. **Learning curves** reflect the phenomenon that is found when the cost to complete a unit is reduced as productivity increases. The possible effect of learning on cost is important for decision making and performance evaluation. Many high-technology companies experience learning effects on costs. These companies compete by learning quickly so they can become a low-cost producer and capture a significant market share.

D.   Some costs have fixed and variable components such as utility cost. These costs are called **semivariable** or mixed.

E.   Other costs are fixed over a small activity range and must increase in amount at designated intervals. These costs are called **semifixed** or step costs. The number of computer operators needed to process input forms is an example of a semifixed cost.

LO4   Describe how managers use cost behavior patterns.

Managers use the cost behavior patterns identified in cost studies to help in the budgeting process.

LO5   Understand how analysts estimate cost behavior using engineering methods and account analysis.

A. The major purpose of cost estimation is to divide total cost into its fixed and variable cost components so predictions can be made. The following expression reflects the basic cost relationship:

$$TC = F + VX$$

where: TC = Total costs
F = Fixed costs
V = Variable costs per unit
X = units of activity

Test Your Understanding

Question: If a company's variable cost per unit is $5 and the total fixed cost for the period is $1,000, what would be the total costs if volume is expected to be 3,000 units?

Answer: At 3,000 units, the variable costs would be $15,000 (3,000 units @ $5 per unit) plus $1,000 for fixed costs, or a total cost of $16,000.

B. When more than one independent variable influences total cost, the relation may be expressed as:

$$TC = F + V_1X_1 + V_2X_2 + ... V_nX_n$$

where F is the fixed cost per period. V_1 is the variable cost per unit of activity X_1 carried out. V_2 is the variable cost per unit of activity X_2 carried out, and so on.

C. Time and motion studies performed by engineers indicate what the cost should be. The **engineering method** of estimating costs is most useful when input/output relationships are well defined and stable over time.

D. Another approach to estimating costs is called **account analysis**. Each element in the chart of accounts is labeled either fixed or variable. Historic records are examined to generate the total fixed costs and variable rate of the period.

LO6   Use historical cost data to estimate cost.

A. Cost behavior of a firm often follows a specific trend. Using past data, future costs can be estimated. This technique allows for adjustments for inflation as well as changes in the relationship between costs and activity. For example, a prior period fixed cost may be changed to the variable cost category based on expected conditions.

B. Steps taken to analyze historic data include: (1) review alternative cost drivers (the independent variable), (2) plot the data, (3) examine the data and method of accumulation.

C. There are several methods used to estimate the historic relationship between costs and activity. **Visual curve fitting** requires the analyst to draw manually a predictor line (through data points) that seems to capture the trend.

D. A variation of visual curve fitting is the **high-low method**, which draws a predictor line based on two representative points. The technique utilizes the point-slope formula, where the change in the dependent variable divided by the change in the independent variable is called the variable rate (or slope). The fixed costs are determined by the line's Y-intercept.

Test Your Understanding

Question: If a company has the following historic information, what would be your estimate for total costs if the company expects to sell 300 units next period?

Units sold	Total costs
200	600
500	1,200

Answer: The variable cost is the change (or slope of the line) which is calculated as follows:

The $\Delta X/\Delta Y$ or ($1,200 - $600)/(500 - 200) = $2 per unit

The fixed cost is calculated by using the formula TC = VC + FC

At the 200 unit level, $600 = ($2)(200) + FC

At the 500 unit level, $1,200 = ($2)(500) + FC

Since both observations are on the same line, the FC is the same amount, or $200.

To estimate the costs at the 300 unit level, use the formula TC = 300($2) + $200

The estimate of total costs at the 300 unit level is $800.

E. A more sophisticated approach to predicting costs uses a statistical analysis called **regression analysis.** This technique fits a trend line through data points using a process called the method of least squares. The method, based on statistical assumption, results in a line that not only helps predict costs but also gives the standard errors of the coefficient and the R-square (R^2). However, the method does require a good understanding of the underlying assumptions, and an analyst should be trained in the technique before applying it in practice.

F. In regression analysis, the R^2 attempts to measure how well the line fits the data. In regression analysis, problems of multicollinearity, heteroscedasticity, and autocorrelation must be considered.

LO7 Explain the costs, benefits, and weaknesses of various cost estimation methods.

A. Whatever method is used to estimate costs, the results will only be as good as the data used.

B. Weaknesses include missing data, outliers, allocated and discretionary costs, inflation, mismatched time periods, and trade-offs in choosing the time period.

C. The engineering method is based on studies of what future costs should be rather than what past costs have been. However, this method is not particularly useful when the physical relation between inputs and outputs is indirect.

D. The account analysis method provides a detailed expert analysis of the cost behavior in each account but it is subjective.

E. The regression method uses all of the observations of the cost data, fits a line statistically to the observations, provides a measure of the goodness of fit and is relatively easy to use with computers and sophisticated calculators. However, the regression model requires that several relatively strict assumptions be satisfied for the results to be valid.

KEY TERMS

LO1 Distinguish between variable costs and fixed costs, and between short run and long run, and define the relevant range.

Cost behavior	The functional relations between changes in activity and changes in cost.
Variable costs (engineered costs)	Costs that change as activity levels change
Fixed costs	Expenditures or expenses that do not vary with volume of activity, at least in the short run.
Short run	The time period during which total productive capacity cannot be changed. Normally this is one year.
Long run	A term denoting a time or time periods in the future, during which total productive capacity can be changed. Normally, this is more than one year.
Relevant range	Activity levels over which costs are linear or for which flexible budget estimates and breakeven charts will remain valid.

LO2 Identify capacity costs, committed costs, and discretionary costs.
capacity.

Capacity costs	Fixed costs incurred to provide a firm with the capacity to produce or to sell.
Committed costs	Costs incurred for the acquisition of long-term activity capacity, usually as a result of strategic planning.
Discretionary costs (programmed costs, managed costs)	Fixed costs not essential for carrying out operations in the short run.

LO3 Understand the nature of various cost behavior patterns.

Curvilinear variable cost	A continuous, but not necessarily linear, function relation between activity levels and costs.
Learning curve (experience curve)	A mathematical expression of the phenomenon that incremental unit costs to produce decrease as managers and labor gain experience from practice.
Semivariable costs	Costs that have both fixed and variable cost components. Also called mixed costs.
Semifixed costs	Costs that increase with activity as a step function.
Marginal cost	The incremental cost or differential cost of the last unit added to production or the first unit subtracted from production.

LO5 Understand how analysts estimate cost behavior using engineering methods and account analysis.

Cost estimation	The process of measuring the functional relation between changes in activity levels and changes in cost.
Engineering method of cost estimation	Estimates of unit costs of product derived from study of the materials, labor, and overhead components of the production process.
Account analysis method	A method of separating fixed from variable costs involving the classification of various product cost accounts.

LO6 Use historical cost data to estimate cost.

Cost driver	A factor that causes an activity's costs or indirectly measures the activity that causes costs.
Independent variable	The variable used to estimate cost behavior in regression analysis.
Dependent variable	In cost estimation, the cost the regression analysis explains.

LO7 Explain the costs, benefits, and weaknesses of various cost estimation methods.

Regression analysis	A method of cost estimation based on statistical techniques for fitting a line to an observed series of data points, usually by minimizing the sum of the squared deviations of the observed data from the fitted line.

Standard errors of the coefficient

A measure of the uncertainty about the magnitude of the estimated parameters of an equation fit with a regression analysis.

t-statistic

For an estimated regression coefficient, the estimated coefficient divided by the standard error of the estimate.

R^2

The proportion of the statistical variance of a dependent variable explained by the equation fit to an independent variable in a regression analysis.

SELF-TEST

LO6   1.   GRAPHING COST BEHAVIOR PATTERNS

Describe the cost behavior pattern reflected in the following graphs:

(a)

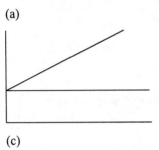

(b)

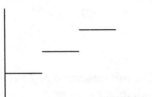

(c)

(d)

a._____

b._____

c._____

d._____

LO6 2. USING THE HIGH-LOW METHOD

Data from the shipping department of Weston Company for the first two months are as follows:

	Number of Packages Shipped	Shipping Department Costs
January	3,500	$5,000
February	4,000	$5,500

REQUIRED:

a. Graph the information using the number of packages shipped as the independent variable.

b. Use the high-low method to calculate the following:

(1) The variable rate

(2) The fixed cost

c. What is the formula for estimating total costs?

d. How does the concept of relevant range affect your prediction of future costs?

LO6   3. INTERPRETING REGRESSION RESULTS

The following output of overhead on direct labor hours was obtained using regression analysis:

Equation:

Intercept	$10,000
Slope	5

Statistical data:

Correlation coefficient	.89
R^2	.79

The company is planning on operating at a level that would call for 3,000 direct labor hours to be utilized for the coming year.

REQUIRED:

a.   Use the regression output to write the overhead cost equation.

b.   Based on the equation, compute the estimated overhead cost for the coming year.

c.   What benefits does regression have over the high-low method?

SOLUTIONS

1. GRAPHING COST BEHAVIOR PATTERNS:

    a. mixed or semivariable
    b. semifixed or step
    c. fixed
    d. variable

2. USING THE HIGH-LOW METHOD:
    a.

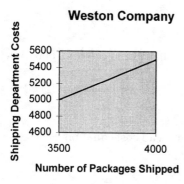

    b. (1) Variable rate   =   change in dependent variable
                                 change in independent variable

                            =   5,500 - 5,000 = 500 = $1/unit shipped
                                4,000 - 3,500   500

(2) Total costs = fixed costs + variable costs

$$TC = FC + (VC)(X)$$

using the higher point:
$5,500 = FC + ($1/unit shipped) (4,000 units)
$5,500 = FC + $4,000
$1,500 = FC

using the lower point:
$5,000 = FC + ($1/unit shipped) (3,500 units)
$5,000 = FC + $3,500
$1,500 = FC

Therefore, fixed costs are $1,500.

c   TC = $1,500 + ($1/unit shipped)(number of units shipped)

d.   Outside this range, the formula may not be valid.

3.   <u>INTERPRETING REGRESSION RESULTS</u>:

a.   TC = $10,000 + $5(Direct labor hours)

b.   TC = $10,000 + $5(3,000) = $25,000

c.   High-low only uses two representative points to estimate the relationship between costs and activity. Regression analysis incorporates all observations in the data set.

STUDY PLAN

1.   Review the learning objectives, exhibits, and key terms for this chapter.

2.   Do Exercise 21 in the text. The problem is similar to the study guide problem. Use the high-low method to confirm your visual estimate.

3.   Try Exercise 20 in the text which integrates your knowledge of the way fixed and variable costs behave when predicting costs in the event of changes in activity levels. Remember the solution to this problem is found at the end of the chapter.

4.   Do Exercise 22 in the text. Can you explain why the variable rate would be different if only June and July data were available? The answer is that two points determine the

prediction line. The observations for June and July together would create a line with a different slope and a different intercept than the data that reflects two other points.

5. Do Exercise 29 in the text. Visual curve fitting can efficiently capture much of the underlying cost relationships without substantial expense incurred by the firm. Then use regression analysis for a more sophisticated predictor line.

6. When a company needs better information about the cost structure, regression is a technique that provides that information. As the manager, it is important that you know how to interpret the results of this statistical method. Do Exercises 30 and 31 in the text to help you understand the output of a regression program.

7. A template is available for Problem 3-33. This is an excellent problem to learn regression using a spreadsheet program.

8. A template is available for Problem 3-24. Learning curves are explained more fully in the appendix of the chapter.

Chapter 4

◆

Cost-Volume-Profit Analysis

This chapter demonstrates how cost, volume, and prices are interrelated. The cost-volume-profit (CVP) model is used to find breakeven and target profit volumes. The margin of safety is defined. The cost-volume-profit model is applied to multiple product cost settings. In addition, the model is shown to be useful in managerial decisions. The CVP model's underlying assumptions and simplifications are highlighted.

LEARNING OBJECTIVES

LO1 Explain how costs, volume, and profits are interrelated.

LO2 List the various applications of the cost-volume-profit model.

LO3 Describe the use of spreadsheets in cost-volume-profit analysis.

LO4 Identify the effects of cost structure and operating leverage on the sensitivity of profit to changes in volume.

LO5 Calculate breakeven using sales dollars as a measure of volume.

LO6 Use the cost-volume-profit model on an after-tax basis.

LO7 Calculate breakeven in a multiproduct setting.

LO8 Define the assumption of the cost-volume-profit model.

TEXTBOOK EXHIBITS

Exhibit 4.1 is the basic cost-volume-profit graph. Note that fixed cost is shown as a horizontal line over the relevant range, variable cost is a sloping line equal to the variable cost per unit rate, sales is a sloping line equal to the sales price per unit. The company breaks even where total costs equal total revenue.

Exhibit 4.2 shows a profit-volume graph. Note the slope of the line is the contribution margin. If no revenue is generated, the company will lose an amount equal to the fixed costs.

Exhibit 4.3 provides a report on four alternatives using sensitivity analysis.

Exhibit 4.4 compares a high fixed cost company with a high variable cost company.

Exhibit 4.5 demonstrates operating leverage.

Exhibits 4.6 through **4.8** provide information for a multiproduct company.

REVIEW OF KEY CONCEPTS

LO1   Explain how costs, volume, and profits are interrelated.

   A.   The cost-volume-profit model is a simple representation of a complex set of relationships. It is essential for managers to understand the relationship among selling prices, unit costs, the volume sold, and profit. Virtually all financial decisions affect costs, volume, or profits.

   B.   Since operating profit is calculated by subtracting total costs from total revenues, the cost-volume-profit equation is described as:

   Operating Profits (Π) = Total Revenues - Total Costs

   or

$$\Pi = PX - (F -+ VX)$$

where,

   P = unit selling price
   X = number of units sold
   V = unit variable costs
   F = fixed operating costs for the period

   C.   Profits calculated using the **C-V-P model** most probably will differ from net income reported using generally accepted accounting principles (GAAP). The C-V-P model reflects variable costing, while GAAP requires the full absorption method.

D.   The contribution concept is particularly important in understanding the C-V-P model. The **contribution margin per unit** is the selling price per unit less the unit's variable costs. (The total contribution margin is calculated by total sales revenues less total variable costs.) The contribution margin represents what is left over from a sale after the variable costs of the sale are considered. The contribution margin conceptually covers fixed costs first, then contributes to the profitability of the company.

E.   The **breakeven point** is the point where total costs and total revenues are equal. At sales activity below this point, the firm will incur a loss. At sales activity above this point, the firm will generate a profit. To determine the breakeven point, substitute zero for the profit figure in the cost-volume-profit equation. Thus, the breakeven point (X) is calculated using this equation:

$$0 = PX - (F + VX)$$

F.   The breakeven equation derived from the cost-volume-profit model is best expressed in a formula format. The breakeven point can be determined by dividing fixed costs per period by the contribution margin per unit.

Test Your Understanding

Question: Assume a company has the following cost structure:

Sales price per unit	$5.00
Variable costs per unit	$2.00
Fixed costs in total	$300.00

How many units must it sell to breakeven?

Answer: 100 units calculated as follows:

Breakeven = Fixed costs/contribution margin
The contribution margin is $3.00 ($5 - $2)
Thus, $300/$3 = 100 units

To prove this, simply reconstruct the income statement using a contribution margin format.

Sales (100 units @ $5)	$500
Variable costs (100 units @ $2)	200
Contribution margin	$300
Fixed costs	300
Operating profit	$0

G. The breakeven formula can be adapted to assist managers in setting volumes that will generate a specific target profit. To modify the formula, treat a target profit as a fixed cost and include it in the numerator of the equation as follows:

$$\text{Volume to earn a specified target profit (lump-sum)} = \frac{\text{Fixed Costs + Target Profit}}{\text{Contribution Margin per Unit}}$$

H. The **profit-volume** model relation is derived from the cost-volume-profit equation. The vertical axis of the profit-volume graph shows the amount of profit or loss for the period. The slope of the line is the contribution margin per unit.

LO2 List the various applications of the cost-volume-profit model.

A. The CVP model can be used to ascertain selling prices to earn a target profit given a specified volume, calculate a new breakeven point if either fixed or variable costs (or both) were to change, and assist in **sensitivity analysis** (what-if assumptions).

B. The CVP model is used to compare **alternatives**.

C. Managers often must consider step fixed costs in the analysis.

D. Another calculation derived from CVP analysis is the **margin of safety.** The margin of safety is the excess of the projected (or actual) sales over the breakeven sales level. It is a measure of how much a forecast can be incorrect and the company still be profitable.

LO3 Describe the use of spreadsheets in cost-volume-profit analysis.

Computer spreadsheets, like Lotus 1-2-3®, and Excel® provide you with considerable additional power in analyzing costs, volume, and profits. Computer spreadsheets also have the capability to graph data.

LO4   Identify the effects of cost structure and operating leverage on the sensitivity of profit to changes in volume.

     A.   The **cost structure** of an organization refers to the proportion of fixed and variable costs to total costs. The extent to which an organization's cost structure is made up of fixed costs is called **operating leverage**.

     B.   Operating leverage is high in firms with a high proportion of fixed costs and a low proportion of variable costs. Since the contribution margin per unit is high for such firms, once the breakeven volume has been reached, profit increases greatly.

Test Your Understanding

Question: Would a new, start up company prefer to have a salesperson on commission or on salary?

Answer? A new company would try to keep its operating leverage low. That is, it would trade off fixed costs, such as a salaried person, for a variable cost, such as a salesperson who receives commission. However, after the company reaches its breakeven point, it might improve profits by hiring salaried individuals and lowering the commission.

LO5   Calculate breakeven using sales dollars as a measure of volume.

The formula to calculate the breakeven sales dollars is:

$$\text{Breakeven Sales Dollars} = \frac{\text{Fixed Costs}}{\text{Contribution Margin Ratio}}$$

If the target profit is a percentage of sales, rather than a lump-sum amount, the formula can be modified by treating the desired profit as a "variable cost." The above formula should be modified as follows:

$$\begin{array}{l}\text{Volume to earn a} \\ \text{specified profit} \\ \text{(\% of sales)}\end{array} = \frac{\text{Fixed Cost}}{\begin{array}{l}\text{Contribution Margin per unit less} \\ \text{(target percentage} \times \text{selling price per unit)}\end{array}}$$

LO6 Use the cost-volume-profit model on an after-tax basis.

The effect of income taxes can be incorporated in the model by substituting after-tax profits for before-tax profits using this relationship:

After-tax Profit = Before-tax Profit multiplied by (1 - Tax Rate)

LO7 Calculate breakeven in a multiproduct setting.

  A. In multiproduct firms, it is more useful to perform breakeven analysis using the contribution margin ratio. The contribution margin ratio is the contribution margin as a percentage of sales.

  B. Multiproduct firms performing C-V-P analysis must make one of four assumptions in order to calculate a breakeven point, namely (1) assume the same contribution margin for all products, (2) assume a fixed product mix, (3) assume a weighted-average contribution margin, or (4) treat each product line as a separate entity.

LO8 Define the assumption of the cost-volume-profit model.

  A. The C-V-P model has three underlying assumptions. The first is total costs are partitioned into fixed and variable components.

  B. The second assumption is cost and revenue behavior is linear throughout the relevant range of activity. That is, fixed costs do not change in total, variable costs per unit remain constant, and the selling price per unit remains constant.

  C. The third assumption is the product mix remains constant throughout the relevant range of activity.

KEY TERMS

LO1 Explain how costs, volume, and profits are interrelated.

Cost-volume-profit model (CVP)	A model that specifies a relation among selling prices, unit costs, volume sold, and profit.
Contribution margin per unit	Selling price less variable costs per unit. The amount each unit contributes to fixed costs and profits.
Breakeven point	The volume of sales required so that total revenues and total costs are equal.
Profit-volume graph	A graph that shows the relation between fixed costs, contribution margin per unit, breakeven point, and sales.
Profit-volume equation	An equation that analyzes changes in volume, contribution margin per unit, or fixed costs on profit.
Margin of safety	The excess of actual, or budgeted, sales over breakeven sales, expressed in dollars or in units of product.
Relevant range	Activity levels over which costs are linear.

LO4 Identify the effects of cost structure and operating leverage on the sensitivity of profit to changes in volume.

Cost structure	The proportion of fixed and variable costs to total costs.
Operating leverage	The tendency of net income to rise at a faster rate than sales when fixed costs are present.
Sensitivity analysis	The study of how the outcome of a decision-making process changes as one or more of the assumptions change.

LO5 Calculate breakeven using sales dollars as a measure of volume.

Contribution margin ratio	Contribution margin divided by net sales.

SELF-TEST

LO1 1. GRAPHING COST-VOLUME-PROFIT RELATIONSHIPS

REQUIRED:

a. Label the points, lines, or areas on the following cost-volume-profit graph:

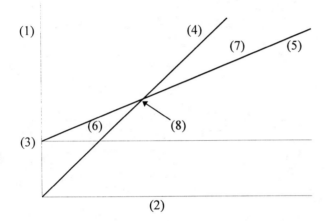

(1)_____   (2)_____

(3)_____   (4)_____

(5)_____   (6)_____

(7)_____   (8)_____

b. Label the points, lines or areas on the following profit-volume graph:

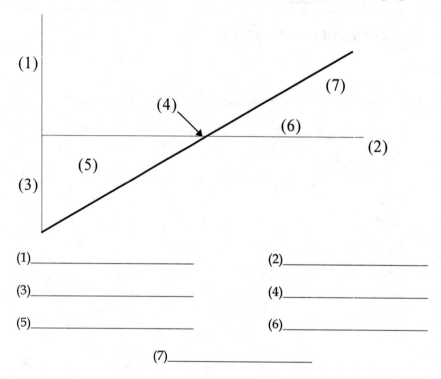

(1)_____   (2)_____

(3)_____   (4)_____

(5)_____   (6)_____

(7)_____

LO1 2. COST-VOLUME PROFIT ANALYSIS

Given for the Laing Company:

Selling price per unit	$9.00
Variable cost per unit	$6.30
Fixed costs per period	$27,000.00

REQUIRED:

a. Breakeven point in units.

b. Breakeven point in sales.

c. Sales that would produce a profit of $9,000.

d. Units needed to breakeven if variable costs increased to $7.00.

e.   Volume needed to earn a 10% return on sales. Show a proof of this calculation.

f.   Selling price to earn a target profit of $10,000 assuming the company expects to sell 12,000 units.

LO3   3.   OPERATING LEVERAGE

A manager is trying to choose between two alternative product lines, A & B. The following information is available:

	A	B
Selling price	$8	$8
Variable costs	$5	$6
Fixed costs	$300	$200
Estimated volume	125 units	150 units

REQUIRED:

a.   Calculate the breakeven point for product A.

b.   Calculate the breakeven point for product B.

c.   What is the margin of safety for product A?

d. What is the margin of safety for product B?

e. What is the expected profit for product A?

f. What is the expected profit for product B?

g. Which company has the higher operating leverage? Why?

LO7   4. BREAKEVEN IN A MULTIPRODUCT SETTING.

A company sells three products, X, Y, and Z. The company has fixed costs in the amount of $2,400. The following information is presented to you:

	X	Y	Z
Price per unit	$10	$5	$7
Variable costs per unit	$6	$2	$6
Number of units sold	1,000	2,000	2,000

REQUIRED:

a. Assuming the product mix will be the same at the breakeven point, compute the breakeven in total units.

b. Assuming the product mix will be the same at the breakeven point, compute the breakeven in units by product line.

c. Assume the product mix will be the same at the breakeven point, compute the sales dollars at breakeven point by product line. (Prepare a contribution format income statement to prove these sales will result in a breakeven position for the company.)

d. Why wouldn't the company breakeven if it sold the 1,000 units of product Z only?

SOLUTIONS

1. <u>GRAPHING COST RELATIONSHIPS</u>

   a. <u>COST-VOLUME-PROFIT GRAPH</u>

1. dollars	5. total costs or variable costs
2. volume	6 loss area
3. fixed costs	7. profit area
4. total revenue	8. breakeven point

   b. <u>VOLUME-PROFIT GRAPH</u>

1. dollars	4. breakeven point
2. volume	5. loss area
3. fixed costs	6. profit area
	7. contribution margin or profit/loss line

2. . <u>COST-VOLUME-PROFIT ANALYSIS</u>:

   a. Breakeven in units $= \dfrac{\text{Fixed costs}}{\text{Contribution margin}} = \dfrac{\$27{,}000}{\$9.00 - \$6.30}$

   $$= \dfrac{\$27{,}000}{\$2.70}$$

   $$= 10{,}000 \text{ units}$$

   b. Breakeven in sales dollars $= \dfrac{\text{Fixed costs}}{\text{Contribution margin ratio}}$

   where the contribution margin ratio $= \dfrac{\text{Contribution margin}}{\text{Sales}}$

   therefore, Breakeven = $\dfrac{\$27{,}000}{(\$2.70/\$9.00)} = \dfrac{\$27{,}000}{0.3} = \$90{,}000$
   in sales

c. Sales to earn a target profit = $\dfrac{\text{Fixed costs + Target profit}}{\text{Contribution margin ratio}}$

$$= \dfrac{\$27{,}000 + \$9{,}000}{0.3} = \dfrac{\$36{,}000}{0.3}$$

$$= \quad \$120{,}000$$

Another way to solve this would be the incremental approach. That is, how many dollars over breakeven does the company need to cover the desired profit of $9,000. Since the contribution margin ratio is 0.3, then $9,000/0.3 = $30,000 additional sales beyond the breakeven point of $90,000, or a total of $120,000.

d. New breakeven = $\dfrac{\text{Fixed costs}}{\text{New contribution margin}}$ = $\dfrac{\$27{,}000}{\$9.00 - \$7.00}$ = 13,500 units

e. Since target profit is a percentage of sales, treat it as a variable cost and reduce the "contribution margin".

Target profit = $\dfrac{\text{Fixed cost}}{\text{Contribution margin - 0.1 (selling price)}}$

$$= \dfrac{\$27{,}000}{\$2.70 - 0.1(\$9)} = \dfrac{\$27{,}000}{\$1.80} = 15{,}000 \text{ units}$$

Proof:

Sales (15,000 units @ $9)	$135,000
Less: Variable cost (15,000 units @ $6.30)	94,500
Contribution margin	$ 40,500
Less: Fixed cost	27,000
Operating profit (10% of sales)	$ 13,500

f. Total revenue = variable cost + fixed cost + profit
(units)(selling price) = units(variable cost) + fixed cost + profit
12,000 (X) = 12,000 ($6.30) + 27,000 + 10,000
12,000 (X) = 75,600 + 27,000 + 10,000
12,000 (X) = 112,600
(X) = 112,600/12,000 or $9.38

3. OPERATING LEVERAGE:

a. $\dfrac{\text{Fixed cost}}{\text{Contribution margin}} = \dfrac{300}{8 - 5} = \dfrac{300}{3} = 100$ units

b. $\dfrac{\text{Fixed cost}}{\text{Contribution margin}} = \dfrac{200}{8 - 6} = \dfrac{200}{2} = 100$ units

c. $\dfrac{\text{Sales - Breakeven sales}}{\text{Sales}} = \dfrac{125 - 100}{125} = \dfrac{25}{125} = 20\%$

d $\dfrac{\text{Sales - Breakeven sales}}{\text{Sales}} = \dfrac{150 - 100}{150} = \dfrac{50}{150} = 33\ 1/3\%$

e.
Sales 125 units @ 8	$1,000
Variable cost 125 units @ 5	(625)
Contribution margin	375
Fixed cost	(300)
Operating profit	$ 75

f.
Sales 150 units @ 8	$1,200
Variable cost 150 units @ 6	(900)
Contribution margin	$ 300
Fixed cost	(200)
Operating profit	$ 100

g. Company A has high operating leverage. Operating leverage is high in firms with a high proportion of fixed costs and a low proportion of variable costs, and results in a high contribution margin per unit. Beyond the breakeven point, company A's profits will increase by its contribution margin per unit, $3, more rapidly than company B when it exceeds its breakeven point. Company B's contribution margin per unit is only $2.

4. <u>BREAKEVEN ANALYSIS IN A MULTIPRODUCT COMPANY</u>:

   a. First compute the weighted-average contribution margin:

	X	Y	Z	
1. Contribution margin	4	3	1	
2. Product mix	100/500	200/500	200/500	
3. Product mix stated as a decimal	.2	.4	.4	
4. (1) times (3)	.8	1.2	.4	
5. Weighted average (sum of line 4)				$2.40

Next, substitute in breakeven formula:

$$\text{Breakeven} = \frac{\text{Fixed costs}}{\text{Weighted-average contribution margin}}$$

$$= \frac{2,400}{2.40} = 1,000 \text{ units}$$

Another way to calculate the weighted average contribution margin is:

	X	Y	Z	
1. Contribution margin	4	3	1	
2. Product mix	1	2	2	
3. Contribution margin for a package of 5 units (1) times (2)	4	6	2	12.0
4. Weighted average (sum of line 3 divided by 5)				$2.40

Note: 5 units are used because the sales mix is 1:2:2. If the sales mix is 2:3:2, for examples, the package would be 7 units.

   b. Number of X units = 0.2 (1,000) = 200 units
       Number of Y units = 0.4 (1,000) = 400 units
       Number of Z units = 0.4 (1,000) = 400 units

c.

	X	Y	Z	Total
Sales	$2,000	$2,000	$2,800	$6,800
Variable costs	1,200	800	2,400	4,400
Contribution margin	$800	$1,200	$400	$2,400
Fixed cost				2,400
Operating profit				$ -0-

d. If 1,000 units of Z were sold, the total contribution margin would only be $1,000 [($7-$6)(1,000 units)]. The company must sell a higher margin unit in order to breakeven.

STUDY PLAN

1. Review the learning objectives, exhibits, and key terms for this chapter.

2. Review the graphs in Exhibit 4.1 and Exhibit 4.2. Be sure you understand that the same information can be presented using these two different formats. The profit-volume graph is more useful in communicating with managers who focus on volume rather than costs, such as marketing managers.

3. Derive the breakeven formula yourself. Begin with the equation format, Profit = Total Revenues - Total Costs. Then substitute zero for Profit. Next, divide total costs into its fixed and variable components. Then show revenue and variable costs as a function of units sold. Finally, define the difference between the selling price and the variable costs per unit as the contribution margin. Your result should be the breakeven formula, X = fixed costs/contribution margin per unit.

4. Do Exercise 18 in the text using the algebraic equation first, then the breakeven formula. You should find the formula approach quicker to use.

5. A template is provided for Problem 4-23. This problem requires that you solve for breakeven in sales dollars.

6. There is a template for Problem 4-24. This problem allows you to see the impact various assumptions have on operating profit.

7. A template is also provided for Problem 4-25. This problem deals with breakeven in a multiproduct organization.

8. There is a template for Problem 4-36. Breakeven is applied to a nonmanufacturing setting. It also addresses the difficulties of breakeven when common fixed costs are allocated to product lines.

Chapter 5

Activity-Based
Management and Costing

This chapter presents the issues in allocating costs to products. Advantages and disadvantages of activity-based costing (ABC) are presented. Using ABC, product costs are calculated. The chapter compares product costing using activity-based costing to traditional cost allocation methods. Examples show the impact of the new production environment on activity bases. Activity-based management and costing can be used to eliminate non-value added costs. Behavioral problems in implementing activity-based costing are identified.

LEARNING OBJECTIVES

LO1   Describe the basic premise of activity-based management.
LO2   Identify strategic uses of activity-based management.
LO3   Relate activity-based management to the value chain.
LO4   Explain how activity-based management can be used to reduce customer response time.
LO5   Understand the concept of activity-based costing.
LO6   Identify the steps in activity-based costing.
LO7   Differentiate among the methods used to allocate costs to products.
LO8   Identify how activity-based management and costing can be used for marketing.
LO9   Explain how the cost hierarchy affects activity-based costing and management.
LO10   Distinguish between resources used and resources supplied.
LO11   Identify advantages of activity based reporting for unused resources.

LO12   Summarize the issues involved in implementing advanced cost-management systems.

TEXTBOOK EXHIBITS

Exhibit 5.1 provides an overview of the value chain.

Exhibit 5.2 presents an analysis of activities cycle.

Exhibit 5.3 depicts elements of customer response time.

Exhibit 5.4 provides examples of cost drivers.

Exhibit 5.5 shows how predetermined overhead rates for activity-based costing are calculated.

Exhibit 5.6 shows how costs are assigned to products using activity-based costing.

Exhibit 5.7 compares activity-based costing with the traditional approach.

Exhibit 5.8 identifies the hierarchy of product costs.

Exhibit 5.9 provides a traditional income statement.

Exhibit 5.10 provides an activity-based management income statement.

REVIEW OF KEY CONCEPTS

LO1   Describe the basic premise of activity-based management.

The basic premise of activity-based management is that products consume activities; activities consume resources. Managers must know (1) the activities that go into making the goods or providing the services, and (2) the cost of those activities.

Test Your Understanding

Question: Identify the activities in a school that consume resources.

Answer: Recruiting new students, registering students, providing research services in the library, teaching classes, processing grades are a few examples.

LO2   Identify strategic uses of activity-based management.

Activity-based management can help a company develop strategies for the company .

Test Your Understanding

Question: Do you think business majors and science majors consume the same resources of the college? How would this affect the strategy of the college.

Answer: It is unlikely science majors and business majors consume similar resources. Science majors may use more of the computer services as well as require more expensive equipment in the teaching of laboratory classes. If a college expands the science major, it can expect over time increased costs in the computer area and in laboratory equipment.

LO3   Relate activity-based management to the value chain.

A. Activity analysis is a fundamental aspect of activity-based management. A value chain is a linked set of value-creating activities leading from raw material sources to the ultimate end use of the goods or services provided.

B. Activity analysis is a systematic way for organizations to evaluate the processes that they use to produce products for their customers and can be used to identify and eliminate activities that add costs but not value to the product.

LO4   Explain how activity-based management can be used to reduce customer response time.

Customer response time can be reduced by identifying the activities that consume the most resources and making them more efficient; and by identifying nonvalue-added activities which can be eliminated.

Test Your Understanding

Question: Assume you order a custom car from an automobile dealer, but are told you would have to wait 4 weeks before the car is shipped from the factory. What nonvalue-added activities do you think the manufacturer could eliminate to improve customer response time?

Answer: Decrease time to place your order, reduce idle time at factory to complete the car according to your specifications, and increase time to deliver the car to you.

LO5   Understand the concept of activity-based costing.

    A. Activity-based costing first assigns costs to activities, then to the products based on each product's use of activities. Activity-based costing focuses attention on the things management can make more efficient or otherwise change.

    B. Traditional costing allocates costs based solely on volume. A predetermined overhead rate is calculated by estimating overhead costs and dividing by estimated volume of the allocation base. In traditional cost systems, the denominator activity is usually direct labor hours, units, or machine hours.

    C. Activity based costing recognizes that the demand for overhead activities is also driven by batch-related and product-sustaining activities.

LO6   Identify the steps in activity-based costing.

    A. Activity-based costing requires accountants to follow four steps: (1) identify the activities that consume resources and assign costs to those activities, (2) identify the cost drivers associated with each activity, (3) compute a cost rate per cost driver unit, and (4) assign cost to products by multiplying the cost driver rate times the volume of cost driver consumed by the product. As a result, several predetermined overhead rates are used, one for each cost driver.

LO7   Differentiate among the methods used to allocate costs to products.

    A. The simplest allocation method for assigning costs to products is one plantwide allocation rate. This considers the entire plant to be one cost pool. The plant may be an entire factory, store, hospital, or other multidepartment segment of a company. The plantwide allocation is appropriate for simple organizations having only a few departments and not much variety in activities in different departments.

Copyright ©1997 Harcourt Brace & Company

B. A more detailed method would treat each department as a cost pool. The company establishes a separate overhead allocation rate or set of rates for each department.

C. Activity-based costing uses a cost pool for each activity.

LO8 Identify how activity-based management and costing can be used for marketing.

Activity-based costing more appropriately identifies the marketing activities needed to service each customer or order. The variability in marketing costs across customer types and distribution channels requires attention by the costing system. Activity-based costing also supports activity-based management by encouraging either the elimination of accounts with high processing costs or better pricing.

LO9 Explain how the cost hierarchy affects activity-based costing and management.

Allocating all costs to units is misleading if some costs do not vary with the volume of unit. When managers are aware of the hierarchy of expenses, namely, capacity-sustaining, product- and customer- sustaining, and batch and unit level cost, they can focus on costs more appropriately.

LO10 Distinguish between resources used and resources supplied.

Resources used for an activity are measured by the cost driver rate times the cost driver volume. Resources supplied to an activity are the expenditure for the activity. Differences between resource usage and the resource supply generally occur because managers have committed to supply certain level of resources before they are used. Activity-based management involves looking for ways to reduce unused capacity.

Test Your Understanding

Suppose your college hired three reference librarians in anticipation of teachers assigning many research projects. However, with the use of the internet, most students are finding less need for reference services. Comment on how the school can use this resource more efficiently.

Comment: Librarians could be used in other parts of the library where more services are required or the college could eliminate the cost of overstaffing.

LO11 Identify advantages of activity-based reporting for unused resources.

    A. Activity-based reports categorizes costs into cost hierarchies so managers can look at the amount of costs in each hierarchy and figure out ways to manage those resources effectively.

    B. The report should highlight how much of the resources for each type of cost are unused.

LO12 Summarize the issues involved in implementing advanced cost-management systems.

    A. Accountants cannot implement activity-based costing without becoming familiar with the operations of the company.

    B. Accountants must become part of a team with management and people from production, engineering, marketing, and other parts of the company.

    C. Top management must support any change in the organization.

KEY TERMS

LO1 Describe the basic premise of activity-based management.

Activity-based costing (ABC)	A method of assigning indirect costs, including nonmanufacturing overhead, to products and services.
Activity-based management (ABM)	The management process that uses the information provided by an activity-based costing analysis to improve organizational profitability.

LO2 Identify strategic uses of activity-based management.

Value chain	A sequence of activities with the objective of providing a product or service to a customer or providing an intermediate food or service in another value chain.

LO6 Identify the steps in activity-based costing.

Cost pool	Grouping of costs.
Cost driver	A factor that causes an activity's costs
Activity center	A unit of the organization that performs a set of tasks.

LO7 Differentiate among the methods used to allocate costs to products.

Plantwide allocation method	Accumulates costs as one cost pool for the entire plant. Then allocates all costs from that pool using a single overhead allocation rate.
Department allocation method	Accumulates cost as cost pools for each department. Then, using separate rates, allocates from each cost pool to products produced in that department.

LO9 Explain how the cost hierarchy affects activity-based costing and management.

Capacity-sustaining activities	Activities that sustain capacity such as plant management.
Product-and customer-sustaining activities	Activities that sustain products and customers such as customer service.
Batch activities	Activities that occur at the batch production level, such as machine setups.
Unit activities	Activities that occur at the unit production level, such as direct materials.

LO10 Distinguish between resources used and resources supplied.

Resources used	Equal the cost driver rate times the cost driver volume.
Resources supplied	The expenditures or the amounts spent on the activity.

LO11 Identify advantages of activity-based reporting for unused resources.

Unused capacity   The difference between resources used and resources supplied.

SELF-TEST

LO6   1. ACTIVITY-BASED COSTING IN A MANUFACTURING ENVIRONMENT

The Englewood Table Company manufactures wooden and plastic tables. The company's Northwestern plant has changed from a labor-intensive operation to a robotics environment. As a result, management is considering changing from a direct-labor based overhead rate to an activity-based cost method. The controller has chosen the following activity cost pools and cost drivers for the factory overhead:

	Overhead Cost	Cost Driver	Expected Annual Cost Driver
Purchase orders	$500,000	number of orders	10,000 orders
Set-up costs	$125,000	number of set-ups	5,000 set-ups
Testing costs	$240,000	number of tests	6,000 tests
Machine maintenance	$260,000	machine hours	10,000 hours

REQUIRED:

a.   Compute the overhead rate for each cost driver.

b.   An order for 100 customized tables had the following requirements:

Number of purchase orders	5
Number of set-ups	10
Number of product tests	75
Machine hours	50

How much overhead would be assigned to this order?

c.   What could management do to reduce the overhead costs assigned to these tables?

LO6   2.   COMPARISON OF ABC WITH TRADITIONAL COSTING

The law firm of Beaver and Smith provides legal services for clients. During the year, corporate clients required 5,000 hours of legal services, while individuals required 2,500 hours. The firm has traditionally used direct labor hours to assign overhead. However, Mr. Beaver believes services to businesses cost more than services to individuals and wishes to adopt activity-based costing. The firm's revenues and costs for the year are shown below:

	Corporate	Individual	Total
Revenue	$500,000	$250,000	$750,000
Expenses:			
Lawyers' salaries	$100,000	75,000	$175,000
Overhead:			
Filing	_____	_____	20,000
Supplies	_____	_____	5,000
Data entry	_____	_____	50,000
Total overhead			$75,000
Total costs	_____	_____	$250,000
Operating profit	=======	=======	$500,000

Mr. Beaver has kept records of the following data for use in the new activity-based costing system:

		Activity Level	
Overhead Cost	Cost Driver	Corporate	Individual
Filing	Number of clients	50	150
Supplies	Number of hours billed	750	250
Data entry	Number of pages entered	2,000	500

Copyright ©1997 Harcourt Brace & Company

REQUIRED:

a. Complete the income statement using the traditional direct-hour allocation base.

	Corporate	Individual	Total
Revenue	$500,000	$250,000	$750,000
Expenses:			
Lawyers' salaries	$100,000	$75,000	$175,000
Overhead	_____	_____	75,000
Total costs	_____	_____	$250,000
Operating profit	=======	======	$500,000

b. Complete the income statement using the three cost drivers in the ABC model.

	Corporate	Individual	Total
Revenue	$500,000	$250,000	$750,000
Expenses:			
Lawyers' salaries	$100,000	$75,000	$175,000
Overhead:			
Filing	_____	_____	20,000
Supplies	_____	_____	5,000
Data entry	_____	_____	50,000
Total costs	_____	_____	$250,000
Operating profit	=======	=======	$500,000

c. How does activity-based costing help the firm manage its costs?

LO10 3. RESOURCES USED VERSUS RESOURCES SUPPLIED

Information about two activities for the Newman Corporation follows:

Resources Used	Cost Driver Rate	Cost Driver Volume
Energy	$10	10 machine hours
Marketing	$20	25 sales calls

Resources Supplied	
Energy	$150
Marketing	$500

Compute unused capacity for energy and marketing

SOLUTIONS

1. <u>ACTIVITY-BASED COSTING IN A MANUFACTURING ENVIRONMENT</u>:

    a.   Purchasing orders:

    $500,000/10,000 = $50 per order

    Set up costs:

    $125,000/5,000 = $25 per set-up

    Product testing:

    $240,000/6,000 = $40 per product test

    Machine costs:

    $260,000/10,000 = $26 per machine hour

    b. Purchasing costs (5 orders x $50 per order) $250
        Set-up costs   (10 set-ups x $25 per set-up) 250
        Product testing (75 tests x $40 per test) 3,000
        Machine costs (50 hours x $26 per machine hour) 1,300
            Total overhead assigned using ABC $4,800

    c. Since product testing and machine costs are the most significant components of the overhead costs, management could reduce the complexity in the design so that less product tests are required. In addition, the product could be redesigned to reduce the number of machine hours assigned to this product. Reducing the number of purchase orders and set-up costs would also reduce the overhead costs, but not significantly.

2. COMPARISON OF ABC WITH TRADITIONAL OVERHEAD COSTING:

a. Income statement using direct-labor allocation:

The overhead rate is computed as follows:

$75,000/7,500 direct labor hours = $10 per hour
Costs assigned to corporate: 5,000 hours x $10 = $50,000
Costs assigned to individual: 2,500 x $10   = 25,000

	Corporate	Individual	Total
Revenue	$500,000	$250,000	$750,000
Expenses:			
Lawyers' salaries	100,000	75,000	$175,000
Overhead	50,000	25,000	75,000
Total costs	$150,000	$100,000	$250,000
Operating profit	$350,000	$150,000	$500,000

b. Income statement using activity-based costing:

Calculation of activity rates:

Filing: $20,000/200 clients = $100 per client
Supplies: $5,000/1,000 hours = $5 per hour
Data entry" $50,000/2,500 pages = $20 per page

	Corporate	Individual	Total
Revenue	$500,000	$250,000	$750,000
Expenses:			
Lawyers' salaries	100,000	75,000	$175,000
Overhead:			
Filing			20,000
$100 x 50	5,000		
$100 x 150		15,000	
Supplies			5,000
$5 x 750	3,750		
$5 x 250		1,250	
Data entry			50,000
$20 x 2,000	40,000		
$20 x 500		10,000	
Total overhead	48,750	26,250	75,000
Total costs	$148,750	$101,250	$250,000
Profit	$351,250	$148,750	$500,000

c. The cost to service corporate clients is slightly higher using ABC than the traditional system. As a result, management may consider pricing their services differently. Alternatively, management could look at the activities that drive the overhead costs to find ways to become more efficient.

3. RESOURCES USED VERSUS RESOURCES SUPPLIED

	Supplied	Used	Unused
Energy	$150	$100	$50
Marketing	$500	$500	$0

STUDY PLAN

1. Review the learning objectives, exhibits, and key terms for this chapter

2. There is a template for Problem 5-28. In nonmanufacturing environments, materials are often included in the overhead costs because they are not significant to the cost of the service. Remember the solution is in the text!

3. There is a template for Problem 5-34. In high-technology manufacturing environments, direct labor has become a very small part of the product cost. In addition, labor is often working at many machines concurrently and no one person's hands are actually on the product. As a result, the cost of labor is classified as overhead. Clearly, direct-labor hours is an inappropriate cost driver for high-technology environments. While some firms have changed to machine hours as the cost driver, this problem demonstrates the detail provided by an activity-based cost system.

4. There is a template for Problem 5-38. You can begin to appreciate the additional amount of effort required for an activity-based costing system as compared to the traditional system.

5. There is a template for Problem 5-40 to help you compute resources used and resources supplied.

Chapter 6

Differential Cost Analysis: Marketing Decisions

This chapter explains how managers use differential costs and revenues to make decisions. These decisions include setting prices. The chapter presents the major influences on pricing and differentiates between short-run and long-run pricing decisions. You will learn what costs are appropriate to use for short-run pricing. You will gain an appreciation for how the value chain and product life-cycle influence long-run decisions. You will become familiar with target costs and target prices as well as learn how to use differential analysis to determine customer profitability.

LEARNING OBJECTIVES

LO1   Understand the differential principle and know how to identify costs for differential analysis.

LO2   Describe the major influences on pricing.

LO3   Differentiate between short-run and long-run pricing decisions.

LO4   Know what costs must be covered by prices.

LO5   Understand how the value chain and product life-cycle influence long-run pricing decisions.

LO6   Understand how to base target costs on target prices.
LO7   Understand how to use differential analysis to determine customer profitability.

TEXTBOOK EXHIBITS

Exhibit 6.1 presents the basic differential analysis model. Note that sales, variable costs, and fixed costs may change between the alternatives.
Exhibit 6.2 presents the differential analysis of a price reduction. Note that since capacity did not change, there were no changes in fixed costs for this example.
Exhibit 6.3 presents the differential analysis of a special order. Again, there were no changes in fixed costs for this example.
Exhibit 6.4 presents information useful for short-run and long-run pricing.
Exhibit 6.5 shows the value chain cost buildup.
Exhibit 6.6 provides a customer profitability analysis.
Exhibit 6.7 provides a format for analyzing a decision to drop a customer.

REVIEW OF KEY CONCEPTS

LO1   Understand the differential principle and know how to identify costs for
        differential analysis.

    A Management decision making is the process of making choices. **Differential analysis** (also known as incremental or marginal analysis) is the analysis of differences among particular alternative actions.

    B. The differential model is an extension of the cost-volume-profit model. However, instead of giving all the elements equal attention, only the differences between alternatives are highlighted. By using the differential approach, managers make more efficient use of their time, especially in complex problems where there are many variables and only a few changes.

    C. In differential analysis, only those elements which change are considered relevant. Differential analysis answers the question, "What activities differ among the alternative?"

    D. Relevant costs are costs that are appropriate for the analysis. It focuses on costs that are differential between the alternatives.

    E. While fixed costs are nearly always differential in long-run decisions involving capacity changes, they are only sometimes differential in short-run operating decisions. In short-run decisions, the manager usually assumes capacity is fixed.

If capacity is increased, or if management decides to increase other fixed costs, then fixed costs are relevant to the analysis.

F. Differential analysis emphasizes cash flows. While the timing of cash flows is very important, differences in the amount of cash flows must be estimated first.

G. Cost and revenue estimates for the status quo are usually more certain than estimates for alternatives. When considering an alternative, the types of activities, the level of activities, and the cost of activities are all estimates subject to error.

Test Your Understanding

Question: A company is considering introducing a new product line. Both products can be produced on the same piece of equipment which must be purchased by the company. Is the new equipment cost relevant to the analysis?

Answer: In comparing each alternative activity to the status quo, the new equipment cost is differential. However, when comparing each alternative activity to each other, the equipment cost would be identical and not differential.

LO2 Describe the major influences on pricing.

Companies have become customer driven, focusing on delivering quality products at competitive prices. The three major influences on pricing decisions are customers, competitors, and costs.

LO3 Differentiate between short-run and long-run pricing decisions.

A. Short-run decisions include pricing for a one-time-only special order with no long-term implications.

B. Long-run decisions include pricing a main product in a major market.
If a firm is to remain in business in the long run, it must recover all of its costs and provide for an adequate return to its owners.

LO4 Know what costs must be covered by prices.

A. In the short-run, a company's minimum price is equal to its short-run differential costs. This is the price at which the company suffers no economic loss.

B.   While the differential approach to pricing presumes that the price must be at least equal to the differential cost of the product, managers may decide to sell a product below its cost for a particular marketing strategy.

C.   For most goods, a sale should at least cover the fixed and variable costs associated with the product, and preferably should contribute to fixed costs and then to the profits of the company. The differential approach leads to correct short-run pricing as long as the company obtains the highest possible price for the unit over its differential costs.

LO5   Understand how the value chain and product life-cycle influence long-run pricing decisions.

A.   The value chain includes the following activities: research and development, design, production, marketing, distribution, and customer service.

B.   The full cost for pricing decisions is justified when a firm enters into a long-term contractual relationship to supply a product, when customized products are developed, and when the company has contracted with a government agency that requires a mark-up on full cost. It is also a useful guide for managers to initially set prices.

C.   The full cost is the total cost of producing and selling a product or service. It includes all the costs incurred by the activities that make up the value chain.

D.   The product life-cycle covers the time from initial research and development to the time at which support to the customer is withdrawn. The term "cradle-to-grave" conveys the sense of capturing all life-cycle costs associated with the product.

LO6   Understand how to base target costs on target prices.

A.   Target costing is the concept of price-based costing (instead of cost-based pricing).

B.   A target price is the estimated price for a product or service that potential customers will be willing to pay.

C.   A target cost is the estimated long-run cost of a product or service that when sold enables the company to achieve targeted profit. Target cost is derived by subtracting the target profit from the target price.

D.   Value engineering is a systematic evaluation of all aspects of research and development, design of products, production, marketing, distribution, and customer service, with the objective of reducing costs while satisfying customer needs.

E.   U.S. laws compel managers to consider costs when setting prices. A business must not engage in predatory pricing. Predatory pricing is deliberately pricing below a product's cost in an effort to drive out competitors.

F.   Under U.S. laws, dumping is also not allowed. Dumping occurs when a foreign company sells a product in the U.S. at a price below the market value in the country of its creation, and this action materially injures (or threatens to materially injure) an industry in the U.S. .

LO7   Understand how to use differential analysis to determine customer profitability.

A.   Companies choose products based on profitability. They also choose customers based on profitability.

B.   Differential costing is useful for deciding which customers a firm should keep and which it should stop servicing.

KEY TERMS

LO1 Understand the differential principle and know how to identify costs for differential analysis.

Differential Analysis	Analysis of differential costs, revenues, profits, investment, cash flows, and the like.
Status quo	Events of costs incurrences that will happen or that a firm expects to happen in the absence of taking some contemplated action.
Relevant cost analysis	Differential cost analysis; identifies the costs (or revenues) relevant to the decision.
Cash flow	Cash receipts minus disbursements from a given asset, or group of assets, for a given period.

Differential cost

The amount of change in cost between two alternatives.

LO5 Understand how the value chain and product life-cycle influence long-run pricing decisions.

Product life cycle

The time from initial research and development to the time at which support to the customer is withdrawn.

LO6 Understand how to base target costs on target prices

Target price

Price based on customers' perceived value for the product and the prices competitors charge.

Target cost

Equals the target price minus desired profit margin

Value engineering

A systematic evaluation of all aspects of research and development, design of products and processes, production, marketing, distribution, and customer service, with the objective of reducing costs while satisfying customer needs.

Predatory pricing

Setting prices deliberately below costs in an effort to drive out competitors.

Dumping

The practice of a foreign company selling a product in the U.S. at a price below the market value in the country of its creation, if this action materially injures (or threatens to materially injure) an industry in the U.S..

SELF-TEST

LO1   1.   DIFFERENTIAL ANALYSIS

A company produces a medical device. The costs of the device at the company's normal volume of 1,000 units per month appear below. Unless otherwise specified, assume a selling price of $500.

Cost data for the product:

Variable manufacturing costs	$180
Fixed manufacturing costs	$100
Variable nonmanufacturing costs	$120
Fixed nonmanufacturing costs	$ 50
Total unit costs	$450

Market research estimates that a price increase to $600 per unit would decrease the monthly volume to 900 units. The accounting department estimates the total variable costs would decrease proportionately with volume and total fixed costs would not change. Would you recommend this action?

LO4   2.   SHORT-RUN PRICING DECISIONS

The Exer Company has the capacity to produce 8,000 units per year. Its predicted operations for the year are:

Sales   6,000 units @ $10 each $60,000

Manufacturing costs:
Variable	$4 per unit
Fixed	$15,000

Marketing & Administrative costs:
Variable	$1 per unit
Fixed	$4,000

REQUIRED:

a.   Prepare a projected income statement for the coming year.

b.   Should the company accept a special order for 1,000 units at a selling price of $8? There are no variable marketing and administrative costs for this order and regular sales will not be affected. What is the impact of this decision on profits?

LO4   3.   DROPPING A PRODUCT LINE

Given for the Essbey Company:

	Ice Cream	Candy	Cards	Total
Sales	$20	$15	$10	$45
Variable costs	10	10	8	28
Contribution Margin	10	5	2	17
Fixed costs (allocated equally to departments)	5	5	5	15
Operating profit	$5	$0	$(3)	$2

REQUIRED:

a.   If no other alternative exists for the Cards department, should the company drop the cards product line? Prepare an income statement showing what would happen to profits if Cards were dropped.

b. Prepare an income statement by product line if Cards were dropped and the common fixed costs were allocated equally to the remaining departments.

c. Referring to part b, above, why did the Candy department go from a "breakeven" position to a loss position? Should it be dropped?

d. What if the common fixed costs were originally allocated $10 to ice cream, $4 to candy and $1 to cards. Would you change any of your decisions? Prepare a revised income statement.

LO6   4.   TARGET COSTS

Wondersigns makes calculators. The company's market research department has discovered a market for a watch-sized calculator which they presently do not make. The watch-sized calculator would likely sell for $5.

Assume the company desires an operating profit of 15%. What is the highest acceptable manufacturing cost for the company to produce the watch-sized calculator?

LO7   5.   CUSTOMER PROFITABILITY

The Richmond Corporation provides management services to three condominiums, Apple Valley, Paradise Village, and Sleepy Hollow. The following presents Richmond Corporation's revenues and costs by customer and is typical for the last few years:

	Apple Valley	Paradise Village	Sleepy Hollow
Revenues	$280	$540	$780
Operating costs:			
Variable costs of services	150	370	550
Fixed general administration	100	100	300
Operating profits	$30	$70	$(70)

Further analysis revealed that the fixed general administration costs include $300 of general expenses allocated equally to the three condominiums. However, Sleepy Hollow has a need for several security guards, who are paid by Richmond Corporation, at a cost of $200.

Required:

Should Richmond Corporation discontinue the Sleepy Hollow account?

SOLUTIONS

1. DIFFERENTIAL COSTS:

Yes, the recommendation is to increase the price of the device to $600. Profits increase by $70,000 calculated as follows:

	Alternative	Status Quo	Difference
Price	$600	$500	
Volume	900	1,000	
Revenue	$540,000	$500,000	$40,000
Variable costs	270,000	300,000	(30,000)
Contribution	$270,000	$200,000	$70,000

Note: Fixed costs do not change and do not have to be included in the analysis since they are not relevant to the analysis.

2. SPECIAL ORDER:

a.
Sales		$60,000
Less variable cost of goods sold:		
Manufacturing	$24,000	
Marketing	6,000	30,000
Contribution margin		30,000
Less fixed costs		
Manufacturing	$15,000	
Marketing	4,000	19,000
Operating profit		$11,000

b. Yes. The contribution margin on this order is $4 ($8 - $4).Thus, the 1000 units would contribute $4,000 (1,000 units @ $4) to the profits of the company. Profits would increase to $15,000.

3. DROPPING A PRODUCT LINE:

a.
Sales ($20 + $15)	$ 35
Less variable costs ($10 + $10)	20
Contribution margin	$15
Less fixed costs	15
Operating profits	$ 0

Copyright ©1997 Harcourt Brace & Company

Profit declined by $2 because the company no longer benefited from the contribution of the Cards Department.

b.

	Ice Cream	Candy
Sales	$20.00	$15.00
Less variable costs	10.00	10.00
Contribution margin	$10.00	$ 5.00
Less fixed costs	7.50	7.50
Operating profits	$ 2.50	$(2.50)

c. Candy contributed $5 to the recovery of fixed costs. The change in profits is due solely to the allocation method and not to any differential cost. Thus, it should not be dropped in the short run.

d.

	Ice Cream	Candy	Cards	Total
Sales	$20	$15	$10	$45
Less variable costs	10	10	8	28
Contribution margin	$10	$ 5	$ 2	$17
Less fixed costs	10	4	1	15
Operating profits	$ 0	$ 1	$ 1	$ 2

No decision would change. The allocation method only affects how the overall profit of $2 is divided among the departments.

4. TARGET COST:

$$\frac{Price}{(Costs + 15\%)} = \frac{\$5}{\$1.15} = \$4.35$$

The highest acceptable manufacturing cost for which the company would be willing to produce the watch-sized calculator is $4.35

5. CUSTOMER PROFITABILITY:

Dropping the Sleepy Hollow account would not save the $100 of fixed costs included in the fixed general administration account. It would only save the security guards' costs and the variable costs of servicing Sleepy Hollow. The following presents a differential analysis comparing the status quo to the alternative of dropping Sleepy Hollow:

	Status Quo	Alternative	Difference
Revenues	$1,600	$820	$780
Operating costs:			
Variable costs of services	1,070	520	550
Fixed general administration	500	300	200
Operating profits	$30	$0	$30

From the above analysis, it is better to keep Sleepy Hollow.

Another way to approach this problem is by focusing on only the relevant elements of the analysis as follows::

	Status Quo	Alternative	Difference
Incremental revenues	$780	$0	$780
Incremental operating costs:			
Variable costs of services	550	0	550
Fixed general administration	200	0	200
Operating profits	$30	$0	$30

This approach highlights that the Sleepy Hollow account provides $30 of operating profits which otherwise would not be generated. The operating loss of $70 reported on the customer profitability income statement is caused by allocating $100 of common costs to the customer. As long as the incremental revenues exceed the incremental costs of servicing Sleepy Hollow, the customer should be retained.

STUDY PLAN

1. Review the learning objectives, exhibits, and key terms for this chapter

2. Redo Self-Study Problem 6.2 in the text focusing only on incremental revenues and incremental costs. Do you see that Jamoca Joe's incremental revenue is $460 and the incremental cost associated with the customer is $425? Thus, if Jamoca Joe is dropped, McKlintoff and Associates would be losing $35 of operating profits generated by this customer. The $40 of fixed expenses allocated to Jamoca Joe's is irrelevant to this analysis.

3. Every special order problem presents its own unique fact pattern. Do a few of the exercises for which the solutions are in the text. Look for incremental revenues and incremental costs in each situation.

4. There is a template for Problem 6-18 in the textbook. This problem allows you to see the relationships among selling prices, costs, volume, and profits. The cost-volume-profit model usually assumes prices do not vary in the relevant range. However, this problem introduces the economic concept that as price increases, quantity demanded decreases.

5. There is a template for Problem 6-28 in the textbook. The problem provides you with an application of target costing.

6. There is a template for Problem 6-29 in the textbook. This special order has several components. Be sure to consider capacity constraints as you solve this problem.

Chapter 7

Differential Cost Analysis: Production

This chapter continues applying differential analysis to management problems and shows how differential cost analysis is applied to production settings. It explains the theory of constraints. The chapter identifies factors associated with make-or-buy decisions and presents a format useful for decisions to sell or process further. You will see formats appropriate for analyzing add-or-drop decisions and identify factors for inventory management decisions.

LEARNING OBJECTIVES

LO1.   Apply differential analysis to product choice decisions.

LO2   Explain and apply the theory of constraints.

LO3   Identify the factors underlying make-or-buy decisions.

LO4   Identify the costs of producing joint products and the relevant costs for decisions to sell or process further.

LO5   Use differential analysis to determine when to add or drop parts of operations

LO6   Identify the factors of inventory management decisions.

LO7   Use linear programming to optimize the use of scarce resources. (Appendix 7.1 in the text).

LO8   Understand the use of the economic order quantity (Appendix 7.2 in the text).

TEXTBOOK EXHIBITS

Exhibit 7.1 shows rationing of scarce capacity. Note while the contribution margin is highest for caramel filled candy, it takes 4 hours of machine time to produce the product line. Thus, because machine capacity is limited, the company is better off producing plain chocolate.

Exhibit 7.2 shows rationing scarce capacity is incorrectly influenced by using absorption unit costs.

Exhibit 7.3 provides a differential analysis for a make-or-buy decision.

Exhibit 7.4 pictures a joint production process. The point at which separate products are identifiable is called the split-off point.

Exhibit 7.5 presents a differential analysis of dropping a product line.

Exhibit 7.6 graphically depicts inventory carrying costs, order costs, and total costs.

Exhibit 7.7 shows how the economic order quantity is calculated.

REVIEW OF KEY CONCEPTS

LO1. Apply differential analysis to product choice decisions.

Product choice decisions are short-run decisions. In the short-run, capacity limitations require choices among options. In the long-run, capacity could change to allow more products to be produced and sold.

LO2 Explain and apply the theory of constraints.

A. The theory of constraints (TOC) is a newly developing management method for dealing with constraints.

B. The TOC focuses on increasing the excess of differential revenue over differential costs when faced with bottlenecks.

C. A **bottleneck** is an operation in which the work to be performed equals or exceeds the available capacity.

D. The **theory of constraints** focuses on three factors: (1) throughput contribution, (2) investments, and (3) other operating costs.

E. **Throughput constraints** are sales dollars minus short-run variable costs.

F. Investments are assets required for production and sales.

G. Other operating costs are all operating costs other than short-run variable costs.

H. The objective of the TOC is to maximize the throughput contributions while minimizing investments and operating costs.

I. In the TOC, bottlenecks must be recognized and found. The needs of the bottleneck resource determine the production schedule of no bottleneck resources. The goal is to increase bottleneck efficiency and capacity.

Test Your Understanding

In The Goal, by Eliyahu Goldratt and Jeff Cox, there is a story about boy scouts on a hike. One scout was very slow so he decided to go to the end of the line to avoid holding others back. As a result, all the scouts in front had no constraints on the pace of their walking. While this formation had the immediate impact that everyone was able to walk at his own pace, the distance between the front and the back of the line increased. Goldratt and Cox argue that resources must be given to the slowest hiker in order to move the entire troop to its destination.

LO3   Identify the factors underlying make-or-buy decisions.

A. A make-or-buy decision occurs when managers must decide whether to meet needs internally or to acquire goods or services from external sources.

B. Factors to consider in a make-or-buy decision include cost factors as well as nonquantitative factors.

C. Nonquantifiable factors include dependability of suppliers and the quality of purchased materials.

D. Make-or-buy decisions also involve long-run strategic decisions since external contractors could raise prices, or the quality of the product as well as the dependability of the suppliers could change in the future.

LO4   Identify the costs of producing joint products and the relevant costs for decisions to sell or process further.

A. In a joint product environment, multiple products are produced from a single production process. The cost incurred up to the split off point is called the joint cost.

B. The splitoff point is the point at which identifiable products emerge and can be separately identified.

C. Costs incurred after the split off point are called additional processing costs.

D. Sell or process further decisions are made in the context of incremental revenues and incremental costs. The common, or joint, cost is irrelevant.

LO5   Use differential analysis to determine when to add or drop parts of operations.

A. Managers must decide when to add or drop products from the product line and when to open or abandon sales territories. While this is another example of a decision that has tremendous long-run implications for the company, the impact of this decision on current profits can also be calculated using differential analysis.

B. Allocated fixed costs that will not be eliminated if the segment is eliminated should not be included in the differential analysis. Allocated fixed costs, which will not change between the alternatives, are not relevant to the analysis.

LO6   Identify the factors of inventory management decisions.

A. Inventory management can also be understood in terms of differential analysis. For inventory, there are two kinds of costs: ordering (set-up) and carrying costs. The total inventory cost is the sum of the carrying and ordering costs.

B. Carrying costs include storage costs, insurance, losses due to inventory damage and theft, property taxes, and the opportunity cost of funds tied up in inventory.

C. The **economic order quantity** (EOQ) is the optimal number of units ordered or produced. The EOQ can be calculated by a formula or by trial and error. Managers should use differential analysis to understand the impact of alternative inventory levels on profits.

D. **Just-in-time** (JIT) inventory is a method of managing purchasing, production, and sales by which the firm attempts to produce each item only as needed for the next step in the production process, or the firm attempts to time purchases so that items arrive just in time for production or sale.

E. JIT practices can reduce inventory levels to zero.

F. JIT is a philosophy rather than a tool or set of tools. The objective is the elimination of all nonvalue-added activities and thus a reduction in cost and time.

G. JIT requires employee involvement and is compatible with the total quality management philosophy.

H. Innovations in inventory management include flexible manufacturing. Companies use flexible manufacturing methods to make production changeovers quickly and reduce set-up costs.

KEY TERMS

LO2 Explain and apply the theory of constraints.

Bottleneck	An operation in which the work to be performed equals or exceeds the available capacity.
Theory of constraints (TOC)	Focuses on revenue and cost management when faced with bottlenecks.
Throughput contribution	Sales dollars minus direct materials costs.
TOC Investments	The assets required for productions and sales.

LO3 Identify the factors underlying make-or-buy decisions.

Make-or-buy decisions	A managerial decision about whether the firm should produce a product internally or purchase it from others. Proper make-or-buy decisions in the short run result when a firm considers only differential costs in decision making.

LO4 Identify the costs of producing joint products and the relevant costs for decisions to sell or process further.

Splitoff point	The point at which individual products emerge from a joint production process.
Joint costs	The costs of simultaneously producing or otherwise acquiring two or more products, called joint products, that a firm must, by the nature of the process, produce or acquire together.
Additional processing costs	The costs incurred in processing joint products after the splitoff point.

LO6 Identify the factors of inventory management decisions.

Setup or order costs	The costs of preparing equipment and facilities so that they can be used for production, or the costs of placing or receiving an order.
Carrying costs	The costs of holding inventory.
Economic order quantity	In mathematical inventory analysis, the optimal amount of stock to order when demand reduces inventory to a level called the reorder point.
Economic order quantity model	The mathematical model used to determine the economic order quantity.
Just-in-time inventory	System of managing inventory for manufacturing where a firm purchases or manufactures each component just before the firm uses it.

SELF-TEST

LO3 1. MAKE-OR-BUY DECISION

Segar Company, a radio manufacturer, is currently producing 5,000 radios a year. It manufactures its own parts and cases. Then it assembles the product. The following are the current costs of the department that manufactures the parts:

Material	$3
Labor	4
Factory overhead, direct	5
Factory overhead, allocated	2
Cost per unit	$14

Another company offered to supply Segar with all the parts it needs at a cost of $13.

REQUIRED:

a. Should Segar buy the parts from outside the company? Assume the facilities would be idle.

b. If Segar could rent the parts department space for $9,000, should it rent the space and buy the parts it needs from the outside vendor?

c. One manager at Segar noted that the factory overhead absorbed by the parts department is $25,000 ($5/unit @ 5,000 units). The manager wants to know how this factor was considered in your analysis.

LO6 2. ECONOMIC ORDER QUANTITY

(Use trial and error)

The Fancy Free Company regularly uses 10 units per day, 300 days per year. Units cost $2 each. Ordering costs are $10 per order and the holding costs of items in inventory are estimated to be 10% of cost per year.

REQUIRED:

a.   Complete the following table:

1. units	100	200	300	500	1000	3000
2. number of orders	_____	_____	_____	_____	_____	_____
3. ordering costs	_____	_____	_____	_____	_____	_____
4. average inventory	_____	_____	_____	_____	_____	_____
5. average cost in inventory	_____	_____	_____	_____	_____	_____
6. carrying costs	_____	_____	_____	_____	_____	_____
7. ordering costs + carrying costs	_____	_____	_____	_____	_____	_____

b.   Compute (or estimate) the economic order quantity.

c.   How many orders will the company place?

SOLUTIONS

1. <u>MAKE-OR-BUY DECISION</u>:

a. No. The incremental costs of materials ($3), labor ($4) and factory overhead ($5), or $12, are less than the suggested $13 price of the part if acquired from the outside vendor. If the company accepts the offer, this year's profits will decrease by $5,000 ($1 per unit @ 5000 units).

b. Yes. The loss of $5,000 will be more than offset by the $9,000 additional revenue. The company's profits will increase by $4,000.

c. Fixed costs were not relevant because they would not change in the short run.

2. <u>ECONOMIC ORDER QUANTITY</u>:

a							
1. units	100	200	300	500	1000	3000
2. number of orders	30	15	10	6	3	1
3. ordering costs	$300	150	100	60	30	10
4. average inventory	50	100	150	250	500	500
5. average cost in inventory	$100	200	300	500	1000	3000
6 carrying costs	10	20	30	50	100	300
7. ordering costs + carrying costs	$310	170	130	110	130	310

b. About 500 units. Using the formula, the EOQ is approximately 548 units.

c. There will be 6 orders.

STUDY PLAN

1. Review the learning objective, exhibits, and key terms for this chapter.

2. The concept of differential analysis is applied to numerous situations concerning production. In all cases, allocated fixed costs are irrelevant in decision-making. Note in Exhibit 7.3 the only relevant component of fixed costs is the incremental fixed cost, such as the salary of an inspector needed only for this product line or the rent on a machine.

3. There are templates for Problems 7-17, 7-18, 7-24, and 7-26.

Chapter 8

◆

Managing Quality and Time

This chapter introduces managing quality and time. You will be able to distinguish between the traditional view of quality and the quality-based view. You will understand why the focus is on the customer. In addition, you will be able to compare with costs of quality control to the costs of failing to control quality as well as understanding why trade-offs in quality control and failure costs are made. You will obtain the tools to identify quality control problems. The chapter provides the rationale why just-in-time concepts and total quality management are tied together. Finally, you learn why time is important in a competitive environment.

LEARNING OBJECTIVES

LO1   Distinguish between the traditional view of quality and the quality-based view.

LO2   Define quality according to the customer.

LO3   Compare costs of quality control to the costs of failing to control quality

LO4   Explain why trade-offs in quality control and failure costs are made.

LO5   Describe the tools to identify quality control problems.

LO6   Explain why just-in-time concepts require total quality management.

LO7   Explain why time is important in a competitive environment.

LO8   Explain how traditional managerial accounting systems support total quality management.

TEXTBOOK EXHIBITS

Exhibit 8.1 compares the "traditional view" of managing quality with the new "quality-based view." Note the assumption underlying the quality-based view is high quality pays for the cost incurred to get it.

Exhibit 8.2 presents some basic examples of performance measures for the three critical success factors: service, quality, and cost.

Exhibit 8.3 presents a cost of quality report. Four categories are highlighted: costs of prevention, appraisal, internal failure costs, and external failure costs. Each expense is shown as a percent of sales.

Exhibit 8.4 shows an example of a control chart. You will see the upper and lower control limits.

Exhibit 8.5 shows a Pareto chart for a company. It identifies several problems and the frequency of occurrence for a period of time.

Exhibit 8.6 shows the components of customer response time.

REVIEW OF KEY CONCEPTS

LO1   Distinguish between the traditional view of quality and the quality-based view.

      A.   Quality is very important in today's competitive environment. Improving quality is a high priority and one of the most important strategic factors affecting companies. **ISO 9000 standards** provide international standards for quality management. These standards are issued by the International Standards Organization (ISO) which is based in Geneva, Switzerland, and are required for products sold to companies in Europe.

      B.   The assumption underlying the **quality-based view** is high quality pays for the cost incurred to get it. As a result, quality can and should always be improved. In comparison, the **traditional-view** assumes there is always a trade-off between the cost of improving quality and maintaining the status quo. The traditional view allowed a minimum level of defective goods to be produced under the belief that the costs to improve quality would outweigh the benefits.

LO2   Define quality according to the customer.

      A.   Many organizations develop performance measures to assess performance of their critical success factors. **Critical success factors** are the elements of performance that are required for success. Three critical success factors that are related to meeting the customer requirements are service, quality, and cost.

B. **Service** refers to the product's tangible and intangible features. Tangible features include how customers are treated by sales people. Service relates to the expectations the customer has about the product's purchase and use. Developing measures of service performance is a major role of management accounting.

C. **Quality** is related to the organization's ability to deliver on its service commitments. One way of looking at quality is giving the customer what was promised in terms of how well the product conforms to specifications.

D. Cost is a function of the organization's ability to efficiently use resources to obtain its objectives.

E. If two products provide the same quality and service, the customer will choose the product with the lower price.

LO3 Compare costs of quality control to the costs of failing to control quality.

A. There are two costs of controlling quality and two costs of failing to control quality.

B. The two costs of controlling quality are (1) prevention costs and (2) appraisal (or detection) costs. **Prevention costs** are costs incurred to prevent defects in the products or services being produced. **Appraisal costs** (also called detection costs) are costs incurred to detect individual units of products that do not conform to specifications.

C. Prevention costs include:
1. Procurement inspection - inspecting production materials upon delivery.
2. Processing control (inspection) - inspecting the production process.
3. Design - designing production procedures to be less susceptible to quality problems.
4. Quality training - training employees to continually improve quality.
5. Machine inspection - ensuring machines are operating properly within specifications.

D.   Appraisal costs, also called detection costs, include:
1. End-process sampling - inspecting a sample of finished goods to ensure quality.
2. Field testing - testing products in use at customer sites.

E.   The two costs of failing to control quality are internal failure costs and external failure costs.

F.   **Internal failure costs** are costs incurred when nonconforming products and services are detected *before* being delivered. Internal failure costs include:
1. Scrap - materials wasted in the production process.
2. Rework - correcting product defects after the product is finished.
3. Reinspection/retesting - quality control testing after rework is performed.

G.   **External failure costs** are costs incurred when nonconforming products and services are detected *after* being delivered to customers. External failure costs include:
1. Warranty repairs - repairing defective products.
2. Product liability - liability to the company resulting from product failure.
3. Marketing costs - marketing necessary to improve company image tarnished from poor product quality.
4. Lost sales - decrease in sales resulting from poor quality products. Customers will go to competitors. (However, the costs reported in this category do not explicitly report the cost of lost business. Only the costs of transactions are included, opportunity costs are normally not recorded in the company's records.)

LO4   Explain why trade-offs in quality control and failure costs are made.

A.   The ultimate goal in implementing a quality improvement program is to achieve zero defects while incurring minimal costs of quality. Managers must make trade-offs between the four cost categories: prevention, appraisal, internal performance and external performance. Total costs of quality must be reduced over time.

B. The costs of quality are often expressed as a percent of sales. A cost of quality report classifies costs as prevention, appraisal, internal performance and external performance, assigns expenses incurred to the categories, and shows the costs incurred as a percent of sales.

LO5 Describe the tools to identify quality control problems.

A. Managers use several tools to identify quality problems. These include control charts, cause and effect analysis, and Pareto charts.

B. Managers rely on signals. A **signal** is information provided to a decision maker. A **warning signal** is a signal that something is wrong and triggers an investigation to find the cause. A **diagnostic signal** suggests what the problem is and perhaps a path to follow in order to solve the problem. Diagnostic signals tend to be more expensive than warning signals, so managers usually rely on warning signals.

C. **Control charts** help managers distinguish between random or routine variations in quality and variations that should be investigated. Control charts show the results of statistical process-control measures for a sample, batch, or some other unit. A specified level of variation may be acceptable, but deviation beyond this level is unacceptable.

D. **Cause and effect analysis** identifies potential causes of defects. This process requires managers to define the effect, such as delivery delays, and then the events that may contribute to the problem (causes). Potential causes can be classified into four categories:
   1. Human factors
   2. Methods and design factors
   3. Machine-related factors
   4. Materials and components factors

E. As prevailing causes are identified, corrective measures are developed and implemented.

F. **Pareto charts** are bar charts that displays the number of problems or defects in a product over time.

LO6   Explain why just-in-time concepts require total quality management.

A.   The just-in-time philosophy is closely linked to total quality management. The objective of **just-in-time** (JIT) philosophy is to purchase goods or to produce goods and services just when needed.

B.   The benefits of just-in-time include reducing or eliminating inventory carrying costs, maintaining high quality standards, and eliminating processes that create defective units.

C.   The following factors are essential for JIT to work:
1.   Total quality. All employees must be involved in quality.
2.   Smooth production flow. Fluctuations in production lead to delays.
3.   Purchasing quality materials. Defective materials disrupts the production flow. Suppliers must be reliable, providing on-time deliveries of high quality materials.
4.   Well-trained, flexible workforce. Workers must be well-trained and also be cross trained to use various machines and work on various parts of the production process.
5.   Backlog of orders. A company needs to have a backlog of orders to keep the production line moving with a JIT system.

D.   Companies have found that JIT requires TQM.

LO7   Explain why time is important in a competitive environment.

A.   Success in competitive markets increasingly demands shorter new-product development time and more rapid response to customers. Response time improvement should be included as a major focus for managers to improve quality. Customer response time is made up of two categories:
1.   New product development time.
2.   Operational measures of time.

B.   **New product development** time is the time period between the first consideration of a product and its delivery to the customer. Firms that respond quickly to customer needs may develop a competitive advantage. **Break-even time** (BET) is the length of time required to recover the investment made in new product development.

C. Break-even time begins when the management approves a project, and, considers the time value of money by discounting all cash flows. Break-even time has several limitations, namely, it ignores all cash flows after the break-even time has been identified, and does not consider strategic and nonfinancial resources for product development. In addition, break-even time varies greatly from one business to the next depending on product life-cycle and investment requirements.

D. **Operational measures of time** indicate the speed and reliability with which organizations supply products and services to customers. Companies generally use two operational measures of time:
    1. Customer response time.
    2. On-time performance.

E. **Customer response time** is the amount of time that elapses from the moment a customer places an order for a product or requests a service to the moment the product or service is delivered to the customer. The quicker the response time, the more competitive the company. Components of customer response time include order receipt time, order waiting time, order manufacturing time, and order delivery time. Usually order receipt time and order delivery time are minimal. Thus, managers usually focus improvement on order waiting time and order manufacturing time.

F. **On-time performance** refers to situations in which product or service is actually delivered at the time it is schedule to be delivered.

LO8 Explain how traditional managerial accounting systems support total quality management.

A. Companies that implement total quality management are likely to find it has little economic benefit unless the company's managerial accounting system supports it. This occurs because managers usually respond to the managerial accounting system instead of the total quality management initiatives.

B. Effective implementation of total quality management requires five changes to traditional managerial accounting systems:
    1. The information should include problem solving information like that coming from control charts and Pareto diagrams, not just financial reports.

2. The workers themselves should collect the information and use it to get feedback and solve problems.

3. The information should be available quickly so workers can get quick feedback.

4. Information should be more detailed than that found in traditional managerial accounting systems.

5. Rewards should be based more on quality and customer satisfaction measures of performance.

KEY TERMS

LO2 Define quality according to the customer.

Service	The product's tangible and intangible features.
Quality	Giving the customer what was promised. How well the product conforms to specifications.

LO3 Compare costs of quality control to the costs of failing to control quality.

Prevention costs	Costs incurred to prevent defects in the products or services being produced.
Appraisal costs (or detection costs)	Costs incurred to detect individual units of products that do not conform to specifications.
Internal failure costs	Costs incurred when nonconforming products and services are detected before being delivered to customers.
External failure costs	Costs incurred when nonconforming products and services are detected after being delivered to customers.

LO5 Describe the tools to identify quality control problems.

Warning signal	Identifies quality control problems by warning there is a problem.

Diagnostic signal	Identities quality control problems by suggesting what the problem is and perhaps a path to follow to solve it.
Control charts	Show the results of statistical process-control measures for a sample, batch, or some other unit.
Cause and effect analysis	Defines the effect and lists events that may contribute to the problems (causes).
Pareto charts	Displays the number of problems or defects in a product over time.

LO6 Explain why just-in-time concepts require total quality management.

New-product development time	The time period between the first consideration of a product and its delivery to the customer.
¯reak-even time (BET)	The length of time required to recover the investment made in new product development.
Operational measures of time	Indicate the speed and reliability with which organizations supply products and services to customers.
Customer response time	The amount of time from when a customer places an order for a product or requests service to when the product or service is delivered to the customer.
On-time performance	Refers to situations in which the product or service is actually delivered at the time it is scheduled to be delivered.

SELF-TEST

LO4   1. COSTS OF QUALITY

Global Industries makes bicycles. The following presents financial information for one year:

Sales	$300,000
Costs:	
Materials inspection	10,000
Scrap	5,000
Employee training	12,000
Returned goods	4,000
Finished goods inspection	18,000
Customer complaints	7,500

Required:

a.   Classify the above items into prevention, appraisal, internal failure, or external failures costs.

1.   Prevention:

2.   Appraisal:

3.   Internal failure:

4.   External failures costs:

b. Create a cost of quality report for the year.

LO 7   2. BREAK-EVEN TIME

Stolling Chairs Company manufactures chairs with wheels. It has just approved a new line of baby strollers scheduled to begin sales in five months. The stroller wheels will require $240,000 investing in new machinery and special tools. The manager has determined that expected production and sales of 150,000 units per year will generate $750,000 discounted cash flow in revenues and $485,000 discounted cash flow in expenses. Calculate the break-even time for the baby stroller line.

LO4   3. QUALITY VERSUS COSTS

Assume a dog food company has discovered a problem involving the mix of ingredients in the dog food mix that costs the company $12,000 in waste and $6,700 in lost business per period. There are two alternative solutions. The first is to lease a new mix processor at a cost of $8,900 per period. The new processor would save the company $11,000 in waste and $5,500 in lost business. The second alternative is to hire additional employee to manually monitor the existing processor at a cost of $3,000 per period. This alternative would save the company $2,000 in waste and $3,200 in lost business per period.

Required: Prepare a differential analysis of the two alternatives. Which alternative should the company choose?

LO4 **4. PARETO CHARTS**

Mr. B's Fast Chicken Restaurant identified the following customer complaints during a given week:

Slow service	6 times
Bad service	10 times
Food cold when delivered to table	8 times
Food spilled when delivered to table	3 times
Wrong order	5 times

Prepare a Pareto chart for Mr. B's for a one-week period.

SOLUTIONS

1. COSTS OF QUALITY:

a. 1. Prevention:
     employee training
     materials inspection

   2. Appraisal:
      finished goods inspection

   3. Internal failure:
      scrap

   4. External failures costs:
      returned goods
      customer complaints

b.

Cost of Quality Report

	Amount	% of Sales
Prevention:		
Employee training	$12,000	4.0%
Materials inspection	10,000	3.3%
Appraisal:		
Finished goods inspection	18,000	6.0%
Internal failure:		
Scrap	5,000	1.7%
External failures costs:		
Returned goods	4,000	1.3%
Customer complaints	7,500	2.5%
Total Costs of Quality	56,500	18.3%

2. BREAK-EVEN TIME:

The break-even time is calculated as:

Investment/net discounted cash flows + Time period from approval to providing product

$240,000/($750,000-$485,000) +   .42 years = 1.32 years

3. QUALITY VERSUS COSTS:

	Present	New Processor	Additional Employees
Waste	$12,000	$ 1,000	$10,000
Lost business	6,700	2,200	3,500
Lease		8,900	
Wages			3,000
Total	$18,700	$12,100	$16,500

The company would prefer leasing the new processor since that is the least cost option.

4. PARETO CHART:

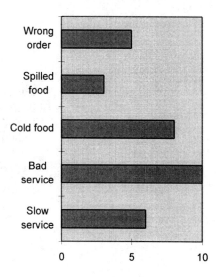

Customer Complaints

STUDY PLAN

1. Review the learning objectives, exhibits, and key terms for this chapter.

2. Try solving the textbook's even numbered Problems 20 - 28. The solutions are found at the end of the text chapter. When you do Problem 28, try using Excel's® chart wizard to create different kinds of bar charts.

3. There is a template for Problem 8-24 in the text. This problem requires you classify the cost of quality into prevention, appraisal, internal and external failure.

4. There is a template for Problem 8-31 in the text. This problem provides you with experience in calculating break-even time.

5. There is a template for Problem 8-38 in the text. The problem requires you to create graphs. This is another good application of the chart wizard function in Excel®.

Chapter 9

◆

Capital Expenditure Decisions

This chapter shifts attention to the long run. We focus on decisions to change operating capacity. Short-run decisions and long-run decisions both rely on a differential analysis of cash inflows and outflows. Long-run capacity decisions involve cash flows over several future periods. This chapter provides insights into the importance of long-term decisions and the appropriate analysis to make economically sound decisions.

LEARNING OBJECTIVES

LO1   Note the separation of the investing and financing aspects of making long-term decisions.

LO2   Summarize the strategic benefits of capital investment.

LO3   Explain why audits are an important step in the capital investment process.

LO4   Identify behavioral issues involved in capital budgeting.

LO5   Describe the steps of the net present value method for making long-term decisions using discounted cash flows. Analyze the effect of income taxes on cash flows.

LO6   Conduct sensitivity analyses of capital budgeting using spreadsheets.

LO7   Apply the internal rate of return method of assessing investment alternatives.

LO8   Explain why discounted cash flow analysis sometimes is not used in making investment decisions.

TEXTBOOK EXHIBITS

Exhibit 9.1 shows the cash flows associated with a new real estate investment proposal. Note the "zero" column represents the beginning of the period. As a result, the $100,000 investment and the initial commissions are already stated in present values.

Exhibit 9.2 expands the first present value analysis. You will see how income taxes are included in the present value calculation. This analysis assumes income taxes are paid at the same time of the inflows and outflows.

Exhibit 9.3 demonstrates how spreadsheets are helpful in doing sensitivity analysis.

Exhibit 9.4 provides an example of the internal rate of return calculation.

REVIEW OF KEY CONCEPTS

LO1   Note the separation of the investing and financing aspects of making long-term decisions.

      A.   Capital budgeting involves deciding which long-term, or capital, investments to undertake and how to finance them. These decisions involve **capital assets**, or long-term assets, that create the fixed, or committed, costs referred to as batch-related, product-related, and process-sustaining costs.

      B.   A company considering acquiring a new plant or equipment must decide first whether to make the investment. Raising the funds required for the investment is a separate decision.

      C.   The premise of separating investment and financing decisions is based on the assumption that when a firm raises funds, the funds are used to support all the firm's assets, or the firm as a whole.

LO2   Summarize the strategic benefits of capital investment.

      A.   The profits from, or the expected cost savings offered by, a capital asset are the most common benefits associated with acquiring capital assets.

      B.   Strategic benefits of capital assets are of increasing importance to companies. Strategic benefits in capital budgeting are difficult to estimate and controversial in including in capital budgeting analyses.

C.   Common strategic benefits that may be provided by capital assets include:
1. Reducing the potential to make mistakes, thus improving the quality of the product.
2. Making goods or delivering a service that competitors cannot make or deliver.
3. Reducing the cycle time to make the product.

LO3   Explain why audits are an important step in the capital investment process.

A.   The accuracy of a capital budgeting model relies heavily on the estimates used in the model. These estimates come from past experience, judgment, or the experience of others.

B.   Comparing estimates to actual results has the following advantages:
1. Audits identify which estimates were wrong so planners can incorporate that knowledge in future estimates to avoid making similar mistakes.
2. Audits can be used to identify and reward those planners who are good at making capital budgeting decisions.
3. Audits create an environment in which planners will not be tempted to inflate their estimates of the benefits.

LO4   Identify behavioral issues involved in capital budgeting.

A.   Recognizing behavioral implications behind the estimates is important in capital budgeting. Factors such as a desire to implement a project or meet performance measures may influence managers' objectivity in making estimates.

B.   Organizational policies, procedures, and performance measures should support accurate estimation because they have an effect on planners when evaluating capital investment projects.

C.   A potential conflict may exist between the criteria used to evaluate individual projects and the criteria used to evaluate an organization's overall performance or the performance of a unit. This may occur as a result of the conflict that exists between the capital budgeting model and the financial accounting reporting model.

LO5 Describe the steps of the net present value method for making long-term decisions using discounted cash flows. Analyze the effect of income taxes on cash flows.

A. **Discounted cash flows** (DCF) methods aid in evaluating investment involving cash flows over time where there is a sufficient time difference between cash payments and receipts. The discounted cash flow methods consider the time value of money.

B. Two discounted cash flow methods are the **net present value** (NPV) method and the **internal rate of return** (IRR) method.

C. Discounted cash flow analysis require the use of a discount rate. The **discount rate** is the interest rate used in computing the present value of the future cash flows. The discount rate for an investment of average risk is the cost of capital of the firm. The appropriate discount rate has three separate elements:
    1. A pure rate of interest reflecting the productive capability of capital assets.
    2. A risk factor reflecting the riskiness of the project.
    3. A premium reflecting inflation expected to occur over the life of the project.

D. Concerning the discount rate:
    1. A **risk free discount rate** includes the pure interest rate and a premium for expected inflation.
    2. The **real interest rate** includes the pure interest rate and a premium for the risk of the investment.
    3. The **nominal interest rate** includes all three factors - pure interest, risk premium, and expected inflation.

E. Steps to compute the net present value include:
    1. Estimate the amounts of future cash inflows and future cash outflows in each period for each alternative under consideration.
    2. Discount the future cash flows to the present using the project's discount rate. The net present value of cash flows of a project is the present value of the cash inflows minus the present value of the cash outflows.
    3. Accept or reject the proposed project or select one from a set of mutually exclusive projects.

F. Decision criteria to accept or reject a proposed project:
    1. If the present value of the future cash flows exceeds the present value of the future cash outflows for a proposal, the firm should accept the alternative because the project will generate a return at least equal to or greater than the minimum desired return.
    2. If the present value of the future cash flows is less than the present value of the future cash outflows for a proposal, that is, the result is a negative number, the firm should reject the alternative. A project with a negative result will not generate the minimum desired return. It may generate a positive return, but it is insufficient.
    3. If the firm must choose one from a set of mutually exclusive alternatives with the same life span, it should select the one with the largest net present value of cash flows.

G. In practice, analysts consider a variety of cash flows. Cash flows associated with investment projects are classified as initial cash flows (at the beginning of the project), periodic cash flows (during the life of the project), and terminal cash flows (at the end of the project).
    1. Initial cash flows include the following:
        a. Outflows:
            1. The cost to acquire the asset. (Remember, financing the asset is a separate decision.)
            2. Freight and installation costs.
        b. Inflows:
            1. The salvage or other disposal value of the existing asset being replaced.
            2. The income tax effect of gain (or loss) on disposal of the existing asset.
            3. Any tax credits on the purchase of the new asset.
            4. The initial working capital required in some situations.
    2. Periodic cash flows include the following:
        a. Outflows:
            1. Opportunity costs (lost "other" inflows) of undertaking this particular project.
            2. Expenditures for fixed and variable production costs.
            3. Expenditures for selling, general, and administrative expenses.
            4. Income tax effects of above outflows.
        b. Inflows:
            1. Receipts from sales (on a cash basis) related to this project.
            2. Savings for fixed and variable production costs.
            3. Income tax effects of above inflows.

Copyright ©1997 Harcourt Brace & Company

3. Terminal cash flows include the following inflows:
   a. Proceeds of salvage of equipment.
   b. Tax on gain or loss on the disposal of the equipment.
   c. The return of working capital in some situations.

LO6 Conduct sensitivity analyses of capital budgeting using spreadsheets.

The calculations of the net present value of a proposed project requires three types of projections or estimates: (1) the amount of future cash flows, (2) the timing of the future cash flows, and (3) the discount rate. Errors in predicting the amounts, timing, or uncertainty of future cash flows will affect the net present value. Computer spreadsheets allow managers to determine the impact of various estimates on the net present value calculation.

LO7 Apply the internal rate of return method of assessing investment alternatives.

A. The **internal rate of return** (IRR) sometimes called the **time-adjusted rate of return,** of a series of cash flows is the discount rate that equates the net present value to zero. It provides managers with the actual rate of return for the project. Spreadsheet programs, and some calculators, can perform this calculation.

B. The decision to accept or reject an investment proposal can be made using either the internal rate of return method or the net present value method. The net present value's decision rule is to accept projects with a positive net present value. The internal rate of return's decision rule is to undertake the investment if its internal rate of return is equal to or greater than the organization's adjusted cost of capital (hurdle rate). If not, reject the investment.

LO8 Explain why discounted cash flow analysis sometimes is not used in making investment decisions.

A. Moving towards computer-integrated-manufacturing systems has changed manufacturing. Companies have found that these high-technology changes, along with revising management accounting systems, provide a competitive edge in the marketplace.

B.   Investments opportunities in technologically advanced systems often show negative net present value calculations. Some of the reasons are:
1. The hurdle rate is too high.
2. There is a bias toward incremental analysis.
3. There is uncertainty about operating cash flows.
4. Managers often exclude benefits that are difficult to quantify. Some of these benefits are:
    a. Greater flexibility in the production process
    b. Shorter cycle times and reduced lead times.
    c. Reduction of nonvalue-added costs.

KEY TERMS

LO1 Note the separation of the investing and financing aspects of making long-term decisions.

Capital budgeting — Involves deciding which long-term, or capital, investments to undertake and how to finance them.

Capital assets — Long-term assets that create the fixed, or committed, costs referred to as batch-related, product-related, and process-sustaining costs.

LO5 Describe the steps of the net present value method for making long-term decisions using discounted cash flows. Analyze the effect of income taxes on cash flows.

Discounted cash flow (DCF) methods — Aid in evaluating investments involving cash flows over time where the time elapsing between cash payment and receipt is significant.

Cost of capital — The cost of acquiring resources for an organization through debt or equity.

Rate of return — Return required by investors to invest in the firm.

Discount rate	The interest rate used in computing the present value of a cash flow; the risk adjusted cost of capital.
Risk-free rate	Includes the pure interest rate and a premium for expected inflation.
Real interest rate	Includes the pure interest rate and a premium for the risk of the investment; does not include expected inflation.
Nominal interest rate	Includes pure interest, risk premium, and expected inflation; used to discount nominal cash flows.
Net present value of cash flows	The present value of the cash inflows minus the present value of the cash outflows.
Initial cash flows	Cash flows occurring at the beginning of the project.
Periodic cash flows	Cash flows occurring during the life of the project.
Terminal cash flows	Cash flows occurring at the end of a project.
Mutually exclusive investments	Selecting any one alternative precludes selecting all others.

LO7   Apply the internal rate of return method of assessing investment alternatives.

Internal rate of return (IRR), or time adjusted rate of return	The discount rate that equates the net present value of the series to zero
Cutoff rate	The risk-adjusted cost of capital; sometimes called the hurdle rate.

SELF-TEST

LO 5   1. COMPUTE THE NET PRESENT VALUE

USE THE FOLLOWING DISCOUNT FACTORS FOR SOLVING THIS EXERCISE:
<u>DISCOUNT FACTORS FOR 10%</u>

PERIOD	PRESENT VALUE OF <u>$1.00</u>	PRESENT VALUE OF $1.00 PER PERIOD RECEIVED AT <u>END OF PERIOD</u>
1	.91	0.91
2	.83	1.74
3	.75	2.49
4	.68	3.17
5	.62	3.79

A firm has an after-tax cost of capital of 10%. It is considering investing in the following projects:

	<u>Project A</u>	<u>Project B</u>
Initial cost	$4,000	$4,000
Periodic cash flows (Received at year-end)		
Year 1	$2,000	$2,000
Year 2	2,000	1,000
Year 3	2,000	3,000
Total	$6,000	$6,000

REQUIRED:

a.   Calculate the net present value of project A. Use the table found at the beginning of this exercise.

b.   Calculate the net present value of project B. Use the table found at the beginning of this exercise.

c.   Both projects cost $4,000 and generate $6,000 of cash flows over the life of the asset. Why are the net present values different?

LO5   2. DISPOSAL OF A CURRENTLY OWNED ASSET

You are given the following present value factors at 8%, the Yontz Company's minimum desired rate of return.

End of Period	Present Value of $1	Present Value of an Annuity of $1
1	0.93	0.93
2	0.86	1.78
3	0.79	2.58
4	0.74	3.31
5	0.68	3.99
6	0.63	4.62

The Yontz Company is considering the replacement of a piece of equipment.   The old machine has a book value of $800 and a remaining estimated life of 5 years with no salvage value at that time. Present salvage value is $200. The new equipment will cost $1,200, including transportation and installation. It has an estimated life of 5 years with no salvage value. Annual cash operating costs are $500 for the old machine and $150 for the new machine.

REQUIRED:

a.   What is the present value of the operating cash outflows for the old machine?

b.   What is the present value of the operating cash outflows for the new machine?

c.   What is the present value of all incremental benefits and operating savings if the new machine is purchased?

d.   What is the differential or incremental investment that is required?

e.   Using a differential approach, what is the net present value of the replacement alternative?

LO6   3. DIFFERENT DISCOUNT RATES

An investment of $3,000 today will yield $1,000 a year at the end of each of the next four years.

REQUIRED: (Use the tables found in the back of the text).

a.   Will the investment be accepted if the cost of capital is 10%?

b.   Will the investment be accepted if the cost of capital is 12%?

c.   Will the investment be accepted if the cost of capital is 20%?

LO7   4. CALCULATE INTERNAL RATE OF RETURN

Each of the two projects requires an investment of $800 in equipment. The firm's cost of capital is 10%. The cash flow patterns and residual (cash) value of equipment are as follows:

Year-end	Cash Flows A	Cash Flows B	Residual Value A	Residual Value B
1	$400	$100	$400	$650
2	400	200	140	550
3	200	200	100	520
4	100	200	-0-	400
5	-0-	300	-0-	200
6	-0-	400	-0-	-0-

REQUIRED:

a. Estimate the internal rate of return by calculating the present value and net present value of each project at each of the following costs of capital: 0, 10, and 20 percent.

b. Calculate the internal rate of return

SOLUTIONS

1.. COMPUTE THE NET PRESENT VALUE:

a Project A.

	Amount	Discount factor	Present Value
1. Initial outlay	(4,000)	1.00	$(4,000)
2. Cash inflows (see below)			
Year 1	2,000	.91	1,820
Year 2	2,000	.83	1,660
Year 3	2,000	.75	1,500
3. Net present value			$ 980

Alternative calculation of cash inflows:

2,000 for 3 years @ 10% = 2,000 (2.49) = 4,980

b. Project B

	Amount	Discount factor	Present Value
1. Initial outlay	(4,000)	1.00	$(4,000)
2. Cash inflows			
Year 1	2,000	.91	1,820
Year 2	1,000	.83	830
Year 3	3,000	.75	2,250
3. Net present value			$ 900

c. The time value of money explains the difference. The project that generates $1,000 more cash in year 2 is worth more to the company because the company can take the cash and invests it in other projects during year 2 is worth more to the company because the company can take the cash, reinvest it, and earn 10% on it.

2. DISPOSAL OF A CURRENTLY OWNED ASSET:

a. PV = $500 x 3.99   = $1,995

b. PV = $150 x 3.99   = $598.50

c. Incremental cash savings   = $350
    Salvage value   = $200
    Present value   = $200 + ($350 x 3.99)
                                    = $200 + $1,396.50
                                    = $1,596.50

d $1,200 - $200 = $1,000

e $1,596.50 - $1,000 = $596.50

3. DIFFERENT DISCOUNT RATES:

a. Yes, the present value is +170. (-3,000 + 3,170)

b. Yes, the present value is + 37. (-3,000 + 3,037)

c. No, the present value is -411. (-3,000 + 2,589)

4. CALCULATING THE INTERNAL RATE OF RETURN

	Year	Interest factor	A	B
At 0%				
	1	1.0	$400	$100
	2	1.0	400	200
	3	1.0	200	200
	4	1.0	100	200
	5	1.0		300
	6		____	400
	Present value		$1,100	$1,400
	Less cost of asset		800	800
	Net present value		$ 300	$ 600

At 10%

1	0.909	$364	$91
2	0.826	330	165
3	0.751	150	150
4	0.683	68	137
5	0.621		186
6	0.564	___	226
Present value		$912	$955
Less cost of asset		800	800
Net present value		$112	$155

At 20%

1	0.833	$333	$83
2	0.694	278	139
3	0.579	116	116
4	0.482	48	96
5	0.402		121
6	0.335	___	134
Present value		$775	$689
Less cost of asset		800	800
Net present value		($25)	($111)

Since the net present value for both alternative is positive at 10% but negative at 20%, the internal rate of return must be between 10 and 20% for both projects.

b.

	A	B
Internal rate of return	18%	15 1/4%

STUDY PLAN

1. Review the learning objectives, exhibits, and key terms for this chapter.

2. Redo Self-Study problem 1 in the text assuming that the cost of capital is changed to 15%. It is important to select the line called "net cash flow". (Now is a good time to learn how to use a computerized spreadsheet software program like Lotus 1-2-3.© or Excel ©.) Would the company accept the project under these new assumptions? The solution is given below.

Cash flow from investment: Year	Amount	Discount Factor	Present Value
0	(60,000)	1.000	(60,000)
1	10,536	870	9,166
2	13,840	.756	10,463
3	15,460	.658	10,173
4	16,660	.572	9,530
5	17,440	.497	8,668
6	21,440	.432	9,262
Operating cash flows			($2,738)

Since the net present value is negative, the company would not accept this investment. The internal rate of return of 14% is not adequate to cover the company's cost of capital of 15%. Only discount rates of 14% or lower will result in the company accepting this investment. Remember, there is some return on this project (14%), however, it is not sufficient if the company sets a minimum return of 15%.

3. There is a template for Problem 9-19 in the text. This is a basic problem demonstrating the impact of the cost of capital on an investment decision. By now you should understand that less cash flows are needed to accept a project at 12% cost of capital than at 20% cost of capital. A higher discount rate makes an investment less attractive.

4. There is a template for Problem 9-21 in the text. This example requires detailed cash flow analysis but ignores income tax considerations.

5. There is a template for Problem 9-23 in the text. You must choose from two mutually exclusive projects.

6. There is a template for Problem 9-29 in the text. This is the most complex of the spreadsheet problems and requires you to consider working capital as well as depreciation in the analysis of an investment decision. In this problem working capital is required in year one in order to maintain desired inventory levels and is returned to the company in year 10 at the end of the project.

Chapter 10

$$\longrightarrow \blacklozenge \longrightarrow$$

Planning and Budgeting

This chapter shows how to develop profit plans. You will gain an appreciation for different types of responsibility centers. The chapter shows you how budgets affect employee motivation and generate potential dilemmas. You will see a master budget and a performance report that compares the master budget to actual performance. You will be able to analyze the differences through the use of variance analysis.

LEARNING OBJECTIVES

LO1 Analyze a budget as a tool for planning and performance evaluation.
LO2 Compare the four types of responsibility centers
LO3 Recognize how a budget can affect employee motivation.
LO4 Describe the master budget.
LO5 Know how to use the budget for performance evaluation.
LO6 Define the different types of variances between actual results and the flexible budget.
LO7 Describe ethical dilemmas in budgeting.
LO8 Develop a comprehensive master budget (Appendix 10.1 in the text).
LO9 Describe an incentive model for accurate reporting (Appendix 10.2 in the text).

TEXTBOOK EXHIBITS

Exhibit 10.1 presents an organization chart for a corporation. Budgeting can begin from the top or from the bottom of an organization.

Exhibit 10.2 presents a sales budget reflecting three possible outcomes. Normally, sales budget contain much of details concerning products and their costs.

Exhibit 10.3 shows overhead which may include variable costs, semivariable or mixed costs, and fixed overhead costs.

Exhibit 10.4 shows a marketing cost budget. Variable selling costs usually vary based on units sold, not units produced.

Exhibit 10.5 provides an example of an administrative cost budget.

Exhibit 10.6 presents a master budget profit plan (a budgeted income statement)

Exhibit 10.7 calculates a sales volume variance by comparing a master budget to a flexible budget. Remember, the flexible budget adjusts the master budget to changes in volume only.

Exhibit 10.8 compares the master budget to actual results and presents the sales volume variance, the sales price variance, as well as production, marketing and administrative cost variances.

Exhibit 10.9 depicts the flexible budget line to highlight differences due to volume compared to price and cost variances.

Exhibits 10.10 through **10. 18** summarize all budgets presented in the chapter.

REVIEW OF KEY CONCEPTS

LO1 Analyze a budget as a tool for planning and performance evaluation.

A. A budget is a comprehensive picture of the expected financial effects of management's decisions on the whole firm. As a **tool for planning**, budgets are usually static. **Static budgets** are budgets for a particular expected level of activity, such as sales or production in units.

B. Budgets provides estimates of expected performance. As a tool for performance evaluation, managers compare expected results to actual results. To be effective as a tool for performance evaluation, managers must develop individual responsibility centers.

C. A **flexible budget** is a budget that reflects different expected levels of activity. A flexible budget has two components: (1) a fixed cost expected to be incurred regardless of the level of activity and (2) a variable cost per unit of activity. While variable costs per unit normally do not change, total variable costs change as the level of activity changes.

LO2   Compare the four types of responsibility centers

    A.   A **responsibility center** is a division or department in a firm responsible for managing a particular group of activities in the organization. Accountants classify responsibility centers according to the activities for which the manager is responsible.

    B.   There are four types of responsibility centers: cost, revenue, profit, and investment.

    C.   **Cost centers** are responsibility centers where management is responsible for costs. There are two kinds of cost centers, based on the types of costs incurred in the center. **Engineered cost centers** have input-output relations sufficiently well-established that a particular set of inputs will provide a predictable and measurable set of outputs, such as production departments. **Discretionary cost centers** are responsibility centers in which input-output relations are not well specified, such as research activities.

    D.   **Revenue centers** are responsibility centers where management is responsible primarily for revenues.

    E.   **Profit centers** are responsibility centers where management is responsible for both revenues and costs.

    F.   **Investment centers** are responsibility centers where management is responsible for revenues, costs and assets.

LO3   Recognize how a budget can affect employee motivation.

    A.   When you assess the effect of budgets or any other part of a motivation system on people, ask the following two questions:

        1.   What types of behavior does the system motivate?
        2.   Is this the desired behavior?

    B.   **Goal congruence** occurs if members of an organization have incentives to perform in the common interest.

LO4   Describe the master budget.

    A.   The master budget is a complete blueprint of the planned operations of the firm for a period.

    B.   The sales budget is the starting point for most master budgets. The chief marketing executive of the firm usually is responsible for preparing the sales budget. The sales budget must be stated in terms of quantities and dollar amounts for each product line.

    C.   The production budget incorporates the production needed to cover the expected sales as well as respond to changes in desired inventory levels.

        1.   Units to be produced can be calculated as follows:

$$\text{Units to be produced} = \text{Number of units to be sold} + \text{Desired units in ending inventory} - \text{Number of units in ending inventory}$$

        2.   Production budgets include estimates of direct materials, direct labor costs, variable and fixed manufacturing overhead costs.

    D.   A budget for marketing and administrative costs must be included in the master budget.

        Note that variable marketing costs usually vary on the units sold, not the units produced.

    E.   **Discretionary fixed costs** are fixed costs that may be changed in the short-run. Many of the so-called fixed costs in the production, marketing, and administrative budgets are discretionary because they are not committed costs which are required to run the firm.

    F.   A master budget includes a profit plan, or budgeted income statement, a budgeted balance sheet, and a cash flow budget.

LO5   Know how to use the budget for performance evaluation.

    A.   Companies use many different methods of providing incentives for both accurate forecasting and good performance.

B. Accountants compare actual results achieved with budgets to derive **variances** for performance evaluation.

LO6 Define the different types of variances between actual results and the flexible budget.

A. A **sales volume variance** is the difference in profits caused by the difference between the master budget sales volume and the actual sales volume. It is calculated by multiplying the difference between the flexible budget and the master budget in units times the contribution margin per unit.

B. A **favorable variance** means that the variance would increase operating profits, holding all other things constant. An **unfavorable variance** would decrease operating profits, holding all other things constant.

C. A detailed explanation of the difference between the master budget and actual performance includes the following variances:
1. Sales volume variance
2. Sales price variance
3. Purchasing and production cost variances
4. Marketing and administrative cost variances

LO7 Describe ethical dilemmas in budgeting.

People in companies face dilemmas all the time. Companies should provide incentives for people to report truthfully. Fraudulent financial reporting often occurs because managers are expected to continually improve operating results.

KEY TERMS

LO1 Understand how to use a budget as a tool for planning and performance evaluation.

Short-term operating budget	Budget that states management's plan of action for the coming year in quantitative terms.
Static budget	A budget developed for a particular level of production or sales.
Flexible budget	A budget that projects receipts and expenditures as a function of activity levels.

LO2 Compare the four types of responsibility centers

Responsibility center	Part or segment of an organization that top management holds accountable for a specified set of activities.
Cost center	A responsibility center that is accountable for expenditures and expenses.
Revenue center	A responsibility center within a firm that is accountable only for revenues generated.
Profit center	A responsibility center that is accountable for both revenues and expenses.
Investment center	A responsibility center, with accountability for revenues, costs, and assets.
Engineered cost centers	Responsibility centers in which input-output relations are sufficiently well established that a particular set of inputs will provide a predictable and measurable set of outputs.

Discretionary cost centers

Responsibility centers in which input-output relations are not well specified.

LO3 Recognize how a budget can affect employee motivation.

Goal congruence

All members of an organization have incentives to perform for a common interest, such as shareholder wealth maximization for a corporation.

LO4 Describe the master budget.

Master budget

A budget projecting all financial statements and their components.

LO6 Define the different types of variances between actual results and the flexible budget.

Variance

The difference between actual and standard costs or between budgeted and actual expenditures, or sometimes, expenses.

Sales volume variance

Budgeted contribution margin per unit multiplied by (planned sales volume less actual sales volume).

Favorable variance

An excess of actual revenues over expected revenues; an excess of standard costs over actual cost.

Unfavorable variance

In standard cost accounting, an excess of expected revenue over actual revenue or an excess of actual cost over standard cost.

Profit variance analysis

Analysis of the causes of the difference between budgeted profit in the master budget and the profits earned.

SELF-TEST

LO4 1. A PRODUCTION BUDGET

Avery Corporation expects to sell 20,000 units of a finished product during the next year. The company began the year with 3,000 units of inventory and wishes to have 2,000 units of finished goods at the end of the year.

REQUIRED:

Prepare a production budget (in units).

LO4 2. A PURCHASE BUDGET

The Avery Corporation in Exercise 1 uses 3 units of raw material X in every finished unit. The company currently has 1,000 units of raw material X on hand and wishes to have 1,500 units in ending inventory. Each unit of X costs $3. (Use your answer from the above Exercise 1.)

REQUIRED:

Prepare a purchase budget for material X.

LO4   3. A CASH BUDGET

The Olympiad Company purchases inventory on account from various suppliers. It normally pays 70% of these in the month purchased, 25% in the first month after purchase and the remaining 5% in the second month after purchase.

Inventory purchased during the first 4 months were as follows:

January	$25,000
February	38,000
March	20,000
April	22,000

REQUIRED:

Prepare a schedule of budgeted cash payments to suppliers for April.

LO6 DEFINE THE DIFFERENT TYPES OF VARIANCES BETWEEN ACTUAL
RESULTS AND THE FLEXIBLE BUDGET.

Biofeed Products provided the following information about its 1994 results (the
company uses FIFO):

	Actual	Master budget
Beginning inventory (200 units)		
Variable costs	$600	$ 600
Fixed costs	$1,000	$1,000
Current manufacturing costs		
(1,000 units actual, 1,200 units budgeted)		
Variable costs	$3,100	$3,600
Fixed costs	$4,900	$4,800
Ending inventory		
(100 actual, 300 budgeted)		
Variable costs	$310	$900
Fixed costs	$490	$1,200

REQUIRED:

a.   Calculate the budgeted cost of goods sold.

b.   Calculate the actual cost of goods sold.

c.   Compute the sales volume variance.

d.   Compute the manufacturing cost variance.

e.   Complete the following chart:

	Actual results: ____ units	Manufac- turing cost variances	Flexible budget: ____ units	Sales volume variance	Master budget: ____ units
Variable costs	_____	_____	_____	_____	_____
Fixed costs	_____	_____	_____	_____	_____
Total costs	_____	_____	_____	_____	_____

f.   The president argues that variances are not fully accounted for because the difference between the budgeted cost of goods sold and the actual cost of goods sold differs from the analysis in part e. Reconcile the difference.

SOLUTIONS

1. A PRODUCTION BUDGET:

Target ending inventory, in units	2,000
Expected sales	20,000
Units needed	22,000
Satisfied from beginning inventory	3,000
Units to be produced	19,000

2. A PURCHASE BUDGET:

Target ending inventory, in units	1,500
Expected production (19,000 @ 3 units of X)	57,000
Units of X needed	58,500
Satisfied from beginning inventory	(1,000)
Units to be purchased	57,500
Cost per unit	$3
Purchase budget	$172,500

3. A CASH BUDGET:

From April purchases ($22,000 @ .70)	$15,400
From March purchases ($20,000 @ .25)	5,000
From February purchases ($38,000 @ .05)	1,900
Total cash paid for purchases	$22,300

4. PREPARING BUDGETS AND DERIVING VARIANCES:

a. Budgeted cost of goods sold:

Beginning inventory	$ 1,600
Budgeted manufacturing costs	8,400
Budgeted goods available	$10,000
Less expected ending inventory	2,100
Budgeted cost of goods sold	$7,900

Calculation of expected ending inventory:

$$\frac{\text{Total budgeted costs}}{\text{Budgeted units produced}} = \frac{\$8,400}{1,200} = \$7.00 \text{ per unit}$$

An alternative calculation of the cost of goods sold:

Units sold from beginning inventory (200 units)	$1,600
Units sold from current production (900 @ $7)	6,300
Cost of goods sold (budgeted)	$7,900

b. Actual cost of goods sold:

Beginning inventory	$1,600
Current manufacturing costs	8,000
Goods available for sale	$9,600
Less ending inventory	800
Total cost of goods sold	$8,800

Calculation of ending inventory:

$$\frac{\text{Total current costs}}{\text{Current units produced}} = \frac{\$8,000}{1,000} = \$8.00 \text{ per unit}$$

An alternative calculation of the cost of goods sold:

Units sold from beginning inventory (200 units)	$1,600
Units sold from current production (900 @ $8)	7,200
Total cost of goods sold (actual)	$8,800

c. Number of units not put into production   200 units
    Budgeted variable cost per unit $3
    Sales volume variance $600 Favorable

Note: The variance is favorable because dollars expected to be spent on variable costs were not spent. However, this reduction in costs is more than offset by revenues not generated as a result of reduced sales levels.

d.

	Actual	Flexible budget for actual	Variance
Variable costs	$3,100	$3,000	$100 U
Fixed costs	4,900	4,800	100 U
Total	$8,000	$7,800	$200 U

e.

	Actual results: 1,000 units	Manufacturing cost variances	Flexible budget: 1,000 units	Sales volume variance	Master budget: 1,200 units
Variable costs	$3,100	$100U	$3,000	$600F	$3,600
Fixed costs	4,900	100U	4,800		4,800
Total costs	$8,000	$200U	$7,800	$600F	$8,400

f. From parts a and b:

	From beginning inventory	From current production	Total
Budgeted cost of goods sold	1,600	$6,300	$7,900
Actual cost of goods sold	1,600	7,200	8,800
Difference	$ -0-	$900 U	$900 U
From part e:			
Master budget	$-0-	$8,400	$8,400
Actual results	-0-	8,000	8,000
Difference	$-0-	$400 F	$400 F

The disparity between the two analyses can be explained by first breaking down the costs into their fixed and variable components:

	Actual	Budgeted	Difference
Variable cost	$3.10	$3.00	$.10 U
Fixed cost per unit	4.90	4.00	.90 U
Total	$8.00	$7.00	$1.00 U

Then, the following chart reconciles the two reports:

	Cost of goods sold from current production (900 units)	Ending inventory (100 units)	Units not produced (200 units)	Total
Master budget				
Variable costs	$2,700	$300	(1) 600	$3,600
Fixed costs	3,600	400	(2) 800	4,800
Total	$6,300	$700	$1,400	$8,400
Adjustment to master budget:				
Variable costs	90U	10U		100U
Fixed costs due to spending too much	90U	10U		100U
Fixed costs due to volume variance	720U	80U		(2)
Sales volume variance	___	___		600 F
Actual results	$7,200	$800		$8,000
Difference	$900 U			$400 F

(1) The sales volume variance is shown as an adjustment from the master budget in explaining the actual results.
(2) The fixed costs that would have been absorbed by the 200 units not produced is not considered in the managerial performance report but it does affect the cost of goods sold reported on the income statement.

STUDY PLAN

1. Review the learning objectives, exhibits, and key terms for this chapter.

2. The text Exercises 12, 13, 15 and 16 are similar to the study guide practice exercises. Try to do these first.

3. There is a template for Problem 10-25 in the text. This problem requires you to prepare a flexible budget.

4. There is a template for Problem 10-32 in the text. This problem is a comprehensive budget problem and requires a detailed performance report.

5. There is a template for Problem 10-37 in the text. This problem requires that you prepare a master budget and a profit variance report (a performance report).

6. There is a template for Problem 10-39 in the text. This problem requires you to use historical information and expected changes to develop the current period's budget. In addition, it requires you to integrate your knowledge of cost-volume-profit relationships to establish prices needed to earn a target operating profit.

Chapter 11

Evaluating Performance

This chapter presents the fundamental variance model that all types of organizations commonly use in one form or another. You will understand the reasons for conducting variance analysis and how to assign responsibility for variances. In manufacturing organizations, detailed variance analysis for variable costs includes separating variances into price and efficiency components. Fixed overhead variance analysis must reflect the special nature of fixed costs. In service organizations, variance analysis also plays a useful role.

LEARNING OBJECTIVES

LO1   Understand the reasons for conducting variance analysis.
LO2   Assign responsibility for variances.
LO3   Separate variances into price and efficiency components.
LO4   Analyze variances using the variable cost variance model.
LO5   Explain why variances occur.
LO6   Analyze overhead variances using the variable cost variation model.
LO7   Calculate fixed cost variances.
LO8   Describe the role of variance analysis in service organizations.
LO9   Summarize how activity-based costing relates to variance analysis.
LO10   Explain how target costing and kaizen costing change the focus of costing systems
LO11   Understand the impact of technology on variance analysis.
LO12   Identify tools managers use to decide when to investigate variances.

LO13   Recognize the relation between actual, budgeted, and applied fixed manufacturing costs. (Appendix 11.1 in the text)

LO14   Calculate the mix variances portion of the efficiency variance (Appendix 11.2 in the text).

TEXTBOOK EXHIBITS

Exhibit 11.1 shows the total variance in operating profits from the original plan. Note the master budget volume is what was expected at the beginning of the period. The flexible budget volume is the actual volume achieved during the period. The sales volume variance is simply the additional contribution margin generated as a result of selling 10,000 additional units.

Exhibit 11.2 shows marketing cost variances including the sales volume variance, the sales price variance, as well as variable and fixed marketing cost variances.

Exhibit 11.3 compares actual costs with a flexible budget, or the standard allowed based on actual production output. For the flexible budget column, note the variable costs change to the actual volume, but fixed costs remain the same, compared to the master budget.

Exhibit 11.4 presents the general model for variance analysis for variable manufacturing costs.

Exhibit 11.5 shows the calculations of variable manufacturing cost variances, using a chart format.

Exhibit 11.6 presents the variable manufacturing overhead variances.

Exhibit 11.7 is a comprehensive profit variance analysis. You will use this format to solve most of the problems in the text.

Exhibit 11.8 is an overview of all of the variances and the units responsible for them.

Exhibit 11.9 applies overhead variance analysis to service organizations.

Exhibit 11.10 demonstrates overhead variance analysis integrated with ABC.

Exhibit 11.11 pictures a labor efficiency variance report that uses a control chart.

REVIEW OF KEY CONCEPTS

LO1   Understand the reasons for conducting variance analysis.

A.   Variance analysis allows managers to investigate the causes of difference from the master budget.

B.   Managers must also decide whether firms need to take corrective steps and whether to reward or penalize employees.

LO2   Assign responsibility for variances.

    A.   Variance calculations are associated with marketing, administration, purchasing and production.

    B.   While there may be interaction effects, variances are calculated for each responsibility center holding all other things constant. Thus, it is possible that a sales volume increase also causes some fixed costs to increase.

    C.   Management usually assigns responsibility for sales volume, sales price, and marketing cost variances to marketing.

    D.   Administrative variances are often the most difficult to manage because they are not *engineered*; that is, there is no well-defined causal relation between administrative input and administrative output.

    E.   Purchasing departments are responsible for purchasing the materials to make products and services. For managerial control, price variances for materials are usually calculated on the quantity purchased, rather than used, during the period.

    F.   The production department assumes responsibility for the fixed manufacturing cost variances and the remaining variable manufacturing cost variances.

LO3   Separate variances into price and efficiency components.

    A.   Accountants generally divide variable manufacturing cost variances into *price* and *efficiency* components.

    B.   A **price variance** measures the difference between the price set as the norm, or standard, and the actual price.

    C.   An **efficiency variance** measures the difference between the actual quantity of inputs used and the standard allowed usage to make the output.

LO4 Analyze variances using the variable cost variance model.

A. The general model for variance analysis can be expressed graphically as follows:

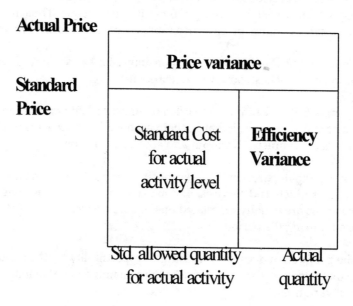

Actual Price

Standard Price

Price variance

Standard Cost for actual activity level

Efficiency Variance

Std. allowed quantity for actual activity

Actual quantity

B. The general model for variance analysis can also be calculated using the following formulas:

Price variance: Actual quantity X Actual price - standard price)
  or,
  AQ (SP - AP)

Efficiency variance: Standard price X (Standard allowed quantity for actual activity - actual quantity),
  or,
  SP (SQ - AQ)

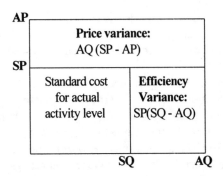

Note: *In variance cost analysis there are two variables: price and quantity. To calculate the price variance, use the actual quantity and vary the price. To calculate the quantity variance, use the standard price and vary the quantity. If you know the four elements, standard price per unit, actual price per unit, standard allowed quantity for actual activity, and the actual quantity used or purchased, you will always be able to calculate these two variances.*

Test Your Understanding

Question: Calculate the price and efficiency variances using the following information:

Standard Price (SP)	$.500
Actual Price (AP)	$.525
Standard Quantity Allowed (SQ)	160,000 lbs.
Actual Quantity Used (AQ)	162,000 lbs.

Answer: The price variance is $4,050U, calculated as follows:
(162,000 lbs.)($.50-$.525).
The efficiency variance is $1,000U, calculated as follows:
($.50)(160,000 - 162,000 lbs.)

Note: *This example uses the same information as direct materials Exhibit 11.5 in the text.*

LO5   Explain why variances occur.

    A.   General reasons for variances.
        1.   Variances occur for many reasons. One explanation of the difference between the predetermined norm or standard and actual results is simply one is expected and the other is actual. Some differences would always be expected.

2. Another reason is the standard may be biased. Some standards are purposely set too loose or tight.

3. Sometimes, there are systematic reasons.

B. Materials and labor variances

1. **Materials price variances** may result from a failure to take purchase discounts, or from using a better or worse grade of raw materials than expected. Alternatively, the price may have changed due to market supply and demand.

2. **Materials efficiency variances** reflect inefficiencies due to inexperienced workers, improperly used materials, and poor quality goods. Sometimes purchasing, not production, causes a materials efficiency variance.

3. **Direct labor price (or wage) variances** occur because managers do not correctly anticipate changes in wage rates.

4. **Direct labor efficiency variances** measure labor productivity. The cause may be workers themselves, that is, poorly motivated or poorly trained. Alternatively, there may be poor materials, faulty equipment, poor supervision, and scheduling problems.

LO6 Analyze overhead variances using the variable cost variation model.

A. Separating variable overhead into price and efficiency components helps managers in their efforts to control overhead costs.

B. Variable overhead variances include the variable overhead price variance and the variable overhead efficiency variance.

C. The **variable overhead price variance** results when the cost per input activity base, for example, machine hours, is either more or less than the actual cost. The formula for calculating the variable overhead price variance is:

Actual quantity X (Actual price times- standard price) , or,
AQ (SP - AP)

D. The **variable overhead efficiency variance** results if the input activity base, for example, machine hours, is different from the standard allowed usage. The formula for calculating the variable overhead efficiency variance is:

Standard price (standard allowed quantity for actual output - actual quantity) , or,

$$SP (SQ - AQ)$$

E.   Managers should interpret variable and overhead price and efficiency variances with care. Accountants sometimes select the input activity base (such as machine hours) without regard to the cause of variable overhead costs.

Test Your Understanding

Question: Calculate the variable overhead price and efficiency variances using the following information:

Standard Price (SP)	$6.8000
Actual Price (AP)	$6.4286
Standard Quantity Allowed (SQ)	2,000 machine hours
Actual Quantity Used (AQ)	2,100 machine hours

Answer: The price variance is $780F, calculated as follows:

(2,100 hrs.)($6.800-$6.4286)

The efficiency variance is $680 calculated as follows:

($6.80)(2,000-2,100 hours)

Note: This example uses the same information as Exhibit 11.6 in the text. Do you understand how the actual rate was calculated? ($13,500/2,100 hours). Also, do you understand why the overhead variances used machine hours, and not units, as the activity measure? Machine hours is an input measure, while units is an output measure!

LO7   Calculate fixed cost variances.

A.   The only fixed cost variances computed for managerial purposes are the price variances (also called spending or budget variances.)

B.   A **fixed overhead price variance** is the difference between actual and budgeted fixed costs.

C.   Because fixed costs do not vary with the measure of activity, there are no efficiency variances for fixed costs.

LO8 Describe the role of variance analysis in service organizations.

Variable overhead often makes up a large portion of the cost of providing services. The overhead analysis model can be applied to service organizations.

LO9 Summarize how activity-based costing relates to variance analysis.
Activity-based costing is commonly used with standard costing. Using activity-based costing, a company has multiple cost drivers. Thus, variance analysis for activity-based costing uses the same approach as for traditional costing, but often has numerous calculations (one for each cost driver).

LO10 Explain how target costing and kaizen costing change the focus of costing systems.

A. Two new approaches to costing are target costing and kaizen costing.

B. **Target costing** is a systematic approach to establishing product cost goals based on market-driven standards. Managers work backwards from the sales price to determine the acceptable costs. The target sales price minus the target margin equals the target cost.

C. **Kaizen costing** supports the cost reduction process in the manufacturing phase of the value chain for *existing* products. "Kaizen" is a Japanese term referring to continuous improvement in relatively small activities rather than major innovative improvement.

LO11 Understand the impact of technology on variance analysis

The variance model in the text generally applies to all types of organizations. However, high-technology firms often have less direct labor and more computerized equipment costs.

LO12 Identify tools managers use to decide when to investigate variances.

A. Managers should investigate a variance on a cost-benefit basis, that is, when the benefits of investigation exceed the costs.

B. The major **cost of variance investigation** is the opportunity cost of employee's time.

C. Quality control techniques rely on the use of **tolerance limits**. Managers can establish tolerance limits based on *statistical confidence limits*.

KEY TERMS

LO3   Separate variances into price and efficiency components.

Price variance

In accounting for standard costs, the difference between actual cost per unit of output (actual price times number of units of input per one unit of output) and standard cost per unit of output, times actual quantity of output.

Efficiency variance

A term used for the quantity variance for materials, labor, or variable overhead in a standard costing system; the difference between actual quantity and standard quantity of inputs, times standard price.

Materials price variance

The difference between actual cost and standard cost of materials, times actual quantity.

Materials efficiency variance

The difference between actual quantity and standard quantity of materials used, times standard price.

Direct labor price (or wage) variance

The difference between actual cost and standard cost of labor, times actual quantity.

Direct labor efficiency variance

The difference between actual quantity and standard quantity of labor used, times standard price.

LO4   Analyze variances using the variable cost variance model.

Variable overhead price variance

The difference between actual cost and standard cost of overhead, times actual quantity.

Variable overhead efficiency variance   The difference between actual quantity and standard quantity of overhead, times standard price.

LO10   Explain how target costing and kaizen costing change the focus of costing systems

Target costing   Establishing the target cost equal to target sales price (market price), minus target margin.

Kaizen costing   A costing system that emphasizes continuous improvement in small activities by seeking to reduce actual costs of production below standard costs.

LO12   Identify tools managers use to decide when to investigate variances.

Variance investigation   Standard cost systems produce variance numbers of various sorts. Management must decide when a variance differs sufficiently from zero to study its cause.

LO13   Recognize the relation between actual, budgeted, and applied fixed manufacturing costs. (Appendix 11.1 in the text)

Production volume variance   Standard fixed overhead rate per unit of estimated volume times (budgeted units minus actual units).

Price variance (spending variance) for fixed manufacturing costs   Actual cost per unit minus standard cost per unit, times actual quantity.

LO14   Calculate the mix variances portion of the efficiency variance (Appendix 11.2 in the text).

Mix variance   The cost difference caused by changing the combination of inputs.

Yield variance   The part of the efficiency variance that is not a mix variance.

SELF-TEST

LO3 1. MATERIAL AND LABOR VARIANCES

The Sandbox Company produces sandboxes. Recently it established standard costs as follows:

Material: 3 pieces per unit at $ .25 per piece.
Labor: .75 hour per unit at $6.00 per hour.

In February, 3,000 pieces of material were purchased for $ .27 per piece. Two thousand five hundred pieces of material were used in producing 800 sandboxes. Labor costs were $3,355 for 550 hours worked.

REQUIRED:

a. Compute the materials price variance.

b. Compute the material efficiency variance.

c. Compute the labor price variance.

d. Compute the labor efficiency variance.

LO6 2. OVERHEAD VARIANCES

The following overhead data for the Jewell Company is presented for analysis of the variances from standard:

Forecast data (expected capacity):

Direct labor hours	20,000
Estimated overhead:	
Fixed	$8,000
Variable	$15,000

Actual results:

Direct labor hours	18,600
Overhead:	
Fixed	$8,060
Variable	$14,030

Allowed or standard hours for actual production, 18,500 hours.

REQUIRED:

a. Calculate the variable overhead spending variance.

b. Calculate the variable overhead efficiency variance.

c. Calculate the fixed overhead price variance.

SOLUTIONS

1. <u>MATERIALS AND LABOR VARIANCES</u>:

    a. AQ (AP - SP)
        3,000 pieces ($ .27 - $ .25)
        $60 Unfavorable

    b. SP (AQ - SQ)
        Standard allowed for actual activity: 800 @ 3 pieces = 2,400
        Therefore, .25 (2,500 - 2,400) = $25 Unfavorable

    c. AQ (AP - SP)
        $3,355/550 hours = $6.10 labor costs per hour
        Therefore, 550 hours ($6.10 - $6.00) = $55 Unfavorable

    d. SP (AQ - SQ)
        Standard allowed for actual activity: 800 @ .75 hour = 600 hours
        Therefore, $6.00 (550 - 600) = $300 Favorable

2. <u>OVERHEAD VARIANCES</u>:

    a. Actual expense - budgeted at actual volume
        $14,030 - $ .75 x 18,600
        $14,030 - $13,950
        $80 Unfavorable

    b. (Actual labor hours - budgeted labor hours) x Standard rate
        (18,600 - 18,500) x $ .75
        $75 Unfavorable

    c. Actual - budgeted
        $8,060 - $8,000
        $60 Unfavorable

STUDY PLAN

1. Review the learning objectives, exhibits, and key terms for this chapter

2. The most difficult concept in calculating the variances is the standard allowed quantity for actual output. This is the flexible budget amount. To calculate the standard allowed quantity, be sure to use the standard input usage per unit of output, such as pounds of materials, or direct labor hours, multiplied by the actual units produced during the period.

3. Look at Exhibit 11.7 in the text. Calculate all variances using the formula approach. For each category, first identify the standard price, the actual price, the standard allowed quantity for actual output, and the actual quantity used. With these four elements, use the formulas:

$$\text{Price variance} = AQ(SP-AP)$$
$$\text{Efficiency variance} = SP(SQ-AQ)$$

Determine if the variance is favorable or unfavorable by comparing the actual result to the standard. For example, direct materials actual price was $.52 and the standard was $.50. Thus, the direct materials price variance is expected to be unfavorable.

Note, the master budget amounts are not relevant in the calculation of purchasing and production variances, marketing and administrative cost variances, and in the sales price variance.

4. There is a template for Problem 11-29 in the text. This problem applies variance analysis in an activity-based cost setting.

5. There is a template for Problem 11-37 in the text. This problem applies variance analysis in a hospital setting.

6. There is a template for Problem 11-38 in the text. You will calculate labor price and efficiency variances.

7. There is a template for Problem 11-46 in the text. This is a comprehensive variance problem which will truly test your understanding of variance analysis. In this problem, the overhead is assigned to products based on direct labor hours. Thus, the direct labor and variable overhead efficiency variances will always vary in the same direction. That is, if direct labor is inefficient, the company must not only incur additional direct labor costs, but also additional variable overhead costs. However, there is no corresponding relationship between the direct labor price and variable overhead price variances.

Chapter 12

◆

Nonfinancial Performance Measures

This chapter discusses innovative ways to evaluate performance "beyond the numbers."

LEARNING OBJECTIVES

LO1   Know how organizations recognize and communicate their responsibilities.
LO2   Understand how the balanced scorecard helps organizations recognize and deal with opposing responsibilities.
LO3   Know how the process of performance improvement works.
LO4   Identify examples of nonfinancial performance measures.
LO5   Explain why employee involvement is important in an effective performance measurement system.

TEXTBOOK EXHIBITS

Exhibit 12.1 presents Johnson & Johnson's code of conduct for its employees.
Exhibit 12.2 provides an example of what is meant by a balanced scorecard.
Exhibit 12.3 lists common benchmark categories.
Exhibit 12.4 shows the value chain.
Exhibit 12.5 lists functional measures of performance.
Exhibit 12.6 lists six worker involvement and commitments.

REVIEW OF KEY CONCEPTS

LO1   Know how organizations recognize and communicate their responsibilities.

Mission statements describe the organization's values, makes specific commitments to those who have an interest in the organization (such as shareholders) , and identifies the major strategies the organization plans to use to achieve its goals. The mission statement communicates an organization's guiding principles, beliefs, and values.

LO2   Understand how the balanced scorecard helps organizations recognize and deal with opposing responsibilities.

The **balanced scorecard** is a set of performance targets and results that show an organization's performance in meeting its objectives relating to its stakeholders. It has been developed and used in many companies. Mostly, the balanced scorecard supports the company's strategic management system.

LO3   Know how the process of performance improvement works.

   A.   Improving performance focuses on recent innovations such as continuous improvement and benchmarking.

   B.   **Continuous improvement** means continuously reevaluating and improving the efficiency of activities. It is the search to (1) improve the activities in which the organization engages through documentation and understanding, (2) eliminate activities that do not add value, and (3) improve the efficiency of activities that are adding value.

   C.   Competitive **benchmarking** involves the search for, and implementation of, the best methods practiced in other organizations or in other parts of one's own organization.

LO4   Identify examples of nonfinancial performance measures.

   A.   The value chain provides a good place to begin identifying the most useful factors to measure. The value chain includes research and development, design, production, marketing, distribution, and customer service.

B. Customer satisfaction measures reflect the performance of the organization on quality control and delivery performance. Examples of such measures include the number of customer complaints and the percentage of on-time deliveries.

C. As well as an external customer focus, an organization must maintain an internal functional performance evaluation. Internal functional performance measures can measure accounting quality, clerical quality, forecasting quality, production control quality, and purchasing quality.

D. The total time it takes to produce a good or service is called **production cycle time**. The cycle time includes processing, moving, storing, and inspecting. As cycle time increases, so do the costs of processing, inspecting, moving, and storage, while service and quality decreases.

E. Production cycle efficiency measures the efficiency of the total production cycle. Production cycle efficiency is calculated as follows:

$$\text{Production cycle Efficiency} = \frac{\text{Processing time}}{\text{Processing time + Moving time + Storage time + Inspection time}}$$

F. Companies are also concerned about environmental issues and attempt to measure their performance and provide incentives for good performance.

LO5 Explain why employee involvement is important in an effective performance measurement system.

A. Many organizations involve workers in creating ideas for improving performance. Competent managers know that workers have good ideas for improving the operations of a company.

B. Worker involvement is important for three reasons:
1. When workers take on real decision-making authority, their commitment to the organization and its goals increases.
2. When decision-making responsibility lies with workers closer to the customer, it leads to more responsive and informed decision making.
3. Giving decision-making responsibility to workers uses their skills and knowledge and provides them with motivation to further develop their skills and knowledge in an effort to improve the organization's performance.

KEY TERMS

LO1   Know how organizations recognize and communicate their responsibilities.

Critical success factors	The factors important for the organization's success.
Stakeholders	Groups or individuals, such as employees, suppliers, customers, shareholders, and the community, who have a stake in what the organization does.

LO2   Understand how the balanced scorecard helps organizations recognize and deal with opposing responsibilities.

Balanced scorecard	A set of performance targets and results that show an organization's performance in meeting its responsibilities to various stakeholders.

LO3   Know how the process of performance improvement works.

Continuous improvement	The continuous reevaluation and improvement of the efficiency of activities.
Benchmarking	Identifying an activity that needs to be improved, finding an organization that is the most efficient at that activity, studying its process, and then utilizing that process.

LO4   Identify examples of nonfinancial performance measures.

Production cycle time	The time involved in processing, moving, storing, and inspecting products and services.
Production cycle efficiency	A measure of the efficiency of the total manufacturing cycle. It equals processing time divided by the manufacturing cycle time.

SELF-TEST

LO4   1.   PRODUCTION CYCLE TIME :

A manufacturing company has the following average times:

Storing	3	hours
Inspection	1	hour
Move time	2	hours
Process time	6	hours

a   Calculate the production cycle time.

b   Calculate the production cycle efficiency

LO4 2. OPERATIONAL PERFORMANCE MEASURES:

The Thomas Company prepares the following operational performance measures for the month of November and December.

Accounting Quality
Operational Performance Measures:
November-December

	November	December
Percent of late reports	3.0%	2.5%
Percent of errors in reports	4.1%	6.3%

REQUIRED:

a. Comment on the operational performance of the accounting department.

b. Why are multiple measures of operational performance useful?

SOLUTIONS

1. PRODUCTION CYCLE TIME AND EFFICIENCY
   a. Production cycle time

Storing	3	hours
Inspection	1	hour
Move time	2	hours
Process time	6	hours
Total production cycle	12	hours

   b. Production cycle efficiency:

   $$\text{Production cycle Efficiency} = \frac{\text{Processing time}}{\text{Processing time} + \text{Moving time} + \text{Storage time} + \text{Inspection time}}$$

   $$= 6/12$$
   $$= 50\%$$

2. OPERATIONAL PERFORMANCE MEASURES:

   a. It appears that while the accounting department has improved performance by reducing late reports, as a result, the reports contain more errors.

   b. Without multiple measures of performance, the company might have been satisfied with the improvement in reducing accounting errors. However, good performance requires error-free reports as well as on-time reports.

STUDY PLAN

1. Review the learning objectives, exhibits, and key terms for this chapter.

2. Concerning production cycle efficiency, note that only process time adds value. Moving time, storing time and inspection time are all nonvalue-added activities.

3. There are no templates for this chapter. The lack of quantitative work in this chapter should not be interpreted as the information in this chapter is less important than the other chapters in the text. Rather, you should gain an appreciation that nonfinancial measures of performance are the most important aspects to consider to improve the organization.

Chapter 13

◆

Divisional Performance Measures and Incentives

Firms rely on their accounting systems to measure performance and to help control and coordinate their activities. This chapter discusses concepts and methods of measuring performance and controlling activities in multidivision companies. Topics include transfer pricing and divisional performance evaluation.

LEARNING OBJECTIVES

LO1   Identify the benefits and disadvantages of decentralization.

LO2   Know the complexities of using return on investment as a divisional performance measure.

LO3   Apply differential analysis to make-or-buy decisions with different transfer prices.

LO4   Discuss transfer pricing issues and methods.

LO5   Discuss multinational transfer pricing rules.

LO6   Identify types of costs to be considered in measuring division operating costs.

LO7   Identify issues in measuring the investment base for return on investment calculation.

LO8   Know the contribution approach alternative to return on investment for division performance measurement.

LO9   Calculate return on investment and identify shortcomings of the measure.

LO10   Calculate residual income.

TEXTBOOK EXHIBITS

Exhibit 13.1 presents a partial organization chart to demonstrate how a company's divisions fit into the entire organization.

Exhibits 13.2 through **13. 5** provide examples for applying differential analysis to make-or-buy decisions involving transfer pricing.

Exhibit 13.6 shows the contribution approach to divisional reporting. Note the product line contribution margin is identified as well as a divisional contribution margin.

REVIEW OF KEY CONCEPTS

LO1   Identify the benefits and disadvantages of decentralization.

    A.   The major advantages of decentralization are:
        1.   Decentralization allows local personnel to respond quickly to a changing environment.
        2.   Decentralization frees top management from detailed operating decisions.
        3.   Decentralization divides large complex problems into manageable pieces.
        4.   Decentralization helps train managers and provides a basis for evaluating their decisions.
        5.   Decentralization motivates managers.

    B.   Decentralization has its disadvantages. Managers may not make decisions in the best interest of the company.

    C.   One objective of decentralization is to create **behavioral congruence** or **goal congruence** to encourage divisional managers to act in ways consistent with organizational goals.

    D.   Managers should distinguish between the measure of an organizational unit's performance and that of the unit manager's performance. Managers often perform well despite the division's poor performance because of factors outside the manager's control.

LO2   Know the complexities of using return on investment as a divisional performance measure

In measuring divisional performance, the concept of divisional operating profits is commonly used. However, it does not consider the investment needed to generate profits. To address this issue, return on investment, ROI, measured on divisional performance is calculated using the following formula:

$$\text{Divisional Return on Investment (ROI)} = \frac{\text{Divisional operating profit}}{\text{Divisional investment}}$$

$$\text{ROI} = \frac{\text{Divisional revenues - Divisional operating costs}}{\text{Divisional investment}}$$

LO3   Apply differential analysis to make-or-buy decisions with different transfer prices.

Transfer price decisions use the same differential analysis which is applied to make or buy decisions.

LO4   Discuss transfer pricing issues and methods.

When goods or services are transferred from one unit of an organization to another, the transaction is recorded in the accounting records. The value assigned to the transaction is called the **transfer price.**

A.   Case 1: Transfer pricing when outside suppliers are available and the selling division is below capacity:

When a selling division has unused capacity, it is normally to the firm's benefit for the buying division to purchase internally. This assumes the differential cost to produce internally is less than the price the outside contractor is charging.

B.   Case 2: Transfer pricing when outside suppliers are available and the selling division is at capacity:

When the selling division is at capacity, there is an opportunity cost for giving up regular sales. Usually, it will not matter whether the buying division buys internally or externally. Similarly, the selling division would be indifferent between selling units inside or outside the organization.

C.   There are three general alternative ways to set transfer prices:
1. Top management intervenes to set the transfer price for each transaction between divisions.
2. Top management establishes transfer price policies that divisions follow.
3   Division managers negotiate transfer prices among themselves.

D.   The disadvantage of **top management intervention** is that top management may become swamped with pricing disputes, and, as a result, division managers will lose flexibility and other advantages of autonomous decision making.

E.   Centrally established transfer price policies should utilize the economic transfer pricing rule. The **economic transfer pricing rule** for making transfers to maximize a company's profits is to transfer at the differential outlay cost to the selling division (typically variable costs) plus the opportunity cost to the company of making the internal transfer ($0 if the seller has idle capacity, and the selling price minus variable costs if the seller is operating at capacity).

F.   Externally based market price-based transfer pricing is generally considered the best basis when there is a competitive market for the product and the market prices are readily available. Market prices are an excellent choice for a transfer price because it represents the price the selling division would receive in an independent transaction. Thus, the selling division is not harmed. The buying division is free to go out into the market and find a better price or buy internally. In the case where there are cost savings by doing business inside the firm, the buying division could benefit from the lower charge.

G.   The basic transfer price rule assumes the company has a measure of differential or variable cost, however, this is not always the case. As a result, full-absorption costs are sometimes used in manufacturing firms as transfer prices

H.   Many companies are implementing activity-based costing to improve the accuracy of costs in cost-based transfer pricing.

I.   Some companies use cost-plus transfer pricing based either on variable costs or full-absorption costs. These methods generally apply a normal markup to costs as a surrogate for market prices when intermediate market prices are not available.

J. If actual costs are used as a basis for the transfer, any variance or inefficiencies in the selling division are passed along to the buying division. Thus, firms use **standard costs** (where available) as the basis for the transfer. This practice promotes responsibility in the selling division and isolates variances within divisions.

K. An alternative to a centrally administered transfer pricing policy is to permit managers to negotiate the price for internally transferred goods and services. The major advantage to **negotiated transfer pricing** is that it preserves the autonomy of the division managers.

L. Under some circumstances the transfer price rule does not provide incentives for the selling division to transfer internally. Firms deal with this situation in several ways: use of cost centers, hybrid centers, dual transfer prices, incentive designs, and negotiated transfer prices.

M. If one division exists solely to support the other divisions of the firm, the selling division could be structured as a cost center.

N. A supplying center that does business with both internal and external customers could be set up as a profit center for external business when the manager has price-setting power, and as a cost center for internal transfers when the managers does not have price-setting power. Performance on external business could be measured as if the center were a profit center, while performance on internal business could be measured as if the center were a cost center.

O. The use of dual transfer prices allow the buying division to be charged with a different price than the selling division recognizes as sales revenue. That is, the buyer could be charged with the cost of the unit, however cost might be determined, and the selling division could be credited with cost plus some profit allowance. This system would preserve cost data for subsequent buyer divisions, and it would encourage internal transfers by providing a profit on such transfers for the selling division.

LO5   Discuss multinational transfer pricing rules

    A.   Global transfer pricing practices include cost based, market based and negotiated transfer prices.

    B.   In international transactions, transfer prices may affect tax liabilities, royalties, and other payments because of different laws in different countries or states.

LO6   Identify types of costs to be considered in measuring division operating costs.

    A.   A key issue in measuring divisional operating costs is to understand how the following costs are treated: (1) controllable and noncontrollable direct operating costs; and (2) controllable and noncontrollable indirect operating costs. In general, direct operating costs, whether controllable or not, are always deducted from divisional revenues in measuring divisional operating profit.

    B.   Indirect costs are charged depending on management's philosophy. Usually, controllable, indirect costs are charged at the market value of the services received.

    C.   Noncontrollable, indirect expenses, such as financing expenses and income taxes, are sometimes charged to divisions so they understand the full cost of their operations to the company. In lieu of actual expenses, some companies charge their divisions with the division's implicit capital. Some arbitrariness occurs whenever indirect expenses are charged.

LO7   Identify issues in measuring the investment base for return on investment calculation.

    A.   When **return on investment** (ROI) is used to evaluate divisions, there are several issues in valuing the denominator of the ROI measure, specifically, what assets are to be included and at what valuation.

    B.   Assets to be included in the investment base should be those under the manager's control and defined consistently throughout the organization.

C. In assigning monetary value to the assets to be included in the investment base, managers can choose historic cost (net of depreciation or at gross book value) or replacement cost (net of replacement cost depreciation or at gross book value).

LO8 Know the contribution approach alternative to return on investment for division performance measurement.

Managers should be careful not to focus on one single statistic like ROI in order to evaluate performance. Multiple performance measures, highlighting contribution margin, controllable operating profit margin, operating profit before interest and income taxes should receive attention. In addition, the impact of allocating the costs of the headquarters must be considered.

LO9 Calculate return on investment and identify shortcomings of the measure.

A. To assist managers in analyzing ROI, the measure can be disaggregated into the **profit margin percentage** and the **investment turnover rate**. As a result, managers can quickly focus in on the problem areas of the division by identifying its profit margin and investment turnover.

B. In establishing the minimum acceptable ROI for divisions, the risks associated with the operation must be considered. A problem associated with the measure is that it can discourage divisions from accepting projects that will increase the company's overall return on investment but bring down a division whose ROI is higher than average. To avoid this consequence, companies may evaluate divisions using residual income. **Residual income** charges a division for the company's cost of capital.

LO10 Calculate residual income

Residual income is defined as:

Residual = Divisional Operating - (Percent Capital Charge x Divisional Investment)
Income   Profits

where the percent capital charge is the minimum acceptable rate of return.

KEY TERMS

LO1 Identify the benefits and disadvantages of decentralization.

Division	A more or less self-contained business unit that is part of a larger family of business units under common control.
Profit center	A responsibility center for which a firm accumulates both revenues and expenses.
Investment center	A responsibility center with control over revenues, costs, and assets.
Decentralize	To give a manager of a business unit responsibility for that unit's revenues, and costs, freeing the manager to make decisions about prices, sources of supply, and the like, as though the unit were a separate business that the manager owns.

LO4 Discuss transfer pricing issues and methods.

Economic transfer pricing rule	Transfer pricing policy where the transfer price is set at the market price or at a small discount from the market price.
Market price-based transfer pricing	Transfer pricing policy where the transfer price is set at the market price or at a small discount from the market price.
Cost-plus transfer pricing	Transfer pricing policy based on full costing or variable costing and actual cost or standard cost plus an allowance for profit.
Dual transfer pricing	Transfer pricing system where the buying division is charged with costs only, and the selling division is credited with cost plus some profit allowance.

Negotiated transfer pricing

System whereby the transfer prices are arrived at through negotiation between managers of buying and selling divisions.

LO9 Calculate return on investment and identify shortcomings of the measure

Profit margin percentage

Indicates the portion of each dollar of revenue that is profit.

Investment turnover ratio

The ratio of divisional sales to the investment in divisional assets

LO10 Calculate residual income

Residual income

The excess of division operating profits over the dollar cost of capital invested in the division.

SELF-TEST

LO3   1. INTRACOMPANY TRANSACTIONS

A divisionalized company has given you the following data:

	DIVISION A	DIVISION B	COMPANY
Sales	$100	$150	$250
Variable costs	60	70	130
Fixed costs	20	30	50
Total costs	$ 80	$100	$180
Operating profit	$ 20	$ 50	$ 70

Both divisions sell 100 units each. Division B is considering enhancing its product to include the product produced by Division A. Thus, it could buy all of Division A's output or buy the 100 units it needs from outside vendors. If Division B sold its products, including the enhancement, the selling price would be $250.

REQUIRED:

a. Prepare an income statement for the divisions and the company if Division B purchased the new parts from Division A at the market price of $1 each. Is the company better off if Division B enhances its product?

	DIVISION A	DIVISION B	COMPANY
Sales	_____	_____	_____
Variable costs	_____	_____	_____
Fixed costs	_____	_____	_____
Total costs	_____	_____	_____
Operating profits	_____	_____	_____

b. The manager of Division B feels the performance of the division would be improved if Division A would sell its product internally at its full cost. Prepare an income statement assuming Division A complied. What happens to the allocation of operating profit between the divisions?

	DIVISION A	DIVISION B	COMPANY
Sales	_____	_____	_____
Variable costs	_____	_____	_____
Fixed costs	_____	_____	_____
Total costs	_____	_____	_____
Operating profits	_____	_____	_____

c. Division A's manager feels it would be in the best long-run interest of the company if Division B buys from Division A. Therefore, the manager is suggesting that Division B buy all of Division A's output at a price of $110. Prepare a revised income statement. What happens to the allocation of operating profits under this method?

	DIVISION A	DIVISION B	COMPANY
Sales	_____	_____	_____
Variable costs	_____	_____	_____
Fixed costs	_____	_____	_____
Total costs	_____	_____	_____
Operating profits	_____	_____	_____

d. What conclusion can you come to concerning transfer prices in divisional organizations?

LO5 2. TRANSFER PRICES AND UNUSED CAPACITY

Newman Company has two decentralized divisions, X and Y. Division X has always purchased certain units from Division Y at $60 per unit. Division Y plans to increase its price to $80. Division X can continue to buy outside at a price of $60. Division Y's costs are:

Y's variable cost	$40
Y's fixed cost	$10,000

REQUIRED:

a.   As manager of Division X, would you buy from Division Y? Why?

b.   Assume Division Y is having trouble selling its product for $80. Should top management require Division X to buy from Division Y?

LO9 3. ROI ANALYSIS:

The following information summarized the operations of William Enterprises for 1994:

	Budget	Actual
Sales	$1,000,000	$1,200,000
Variable expenses	(400,000)	(456,000)
Fixed expenses	(500,000)	(600,000)
Income before taxes	$100,000	$144,000
Average total assets	$500,000	$800,000

REQUIRED:

Present a comparative analysis for budgeted and actual ROI that indicates the ROI measure is a product of asset turnover and profit margin.

SOLUTIONS

1. INTRACOMPANY TRANSACTIONS:

a.

	DIVISION A	DIVISION B	COMPANY
Sales	$100	$250	$350
Variable costs	60	170	230
Fixed costs	20	30	50
Total costs	$ 80	$200	$280
Operating profit	$ 20	$ 50	$ 70

The company would be in the same position if Division A sold its output to Division B or to outsiders. Division B's new product generates incremental revenues of $100 and the market price of its incremental cost is $100.

b.

	DIVISION A	DIVISION B	COMPANY
Sales	$80	$250	$330
Variable costs	60	150	210
Fixed costs	20	30	50
Total costs	$ 80	$180	$260
Operating profit	$ 0	$ 70	$ 70

All of the $70 profit is allocated to Division B.

c.

	DIVISION A	DIVISION B	COMPANY
Sales	$110	$250	$360
Variable costs	60	180	240
Fixed costs	20	30	50
Total costs	$ 80	$210	$290
Operating profit	$ 30	$ 40	$ 70

$30 profit is allocated to Division A, $40 profit is allocated to Division B.

d. Transfer prices affect the allocation of profits between divisions.

2. TRANSFER PRICES AND UNUSED CAPACITY:

a. No. If Division X is evaluated on operating profit, buying at $80 rather than $60 will reduce performance.

b. To improve the profit of the company as a whole, Division X should buy from Division Y because the incremental cost to produce a unit is only $40 as opposed to the cost to buy outside of $60. Thus, the company as a whole would be better off by $20 for each unit Division X buys from Division Y. However, if top management imposes a decision on the managers, hostility may be created. This might be a situation where dual transfer prices are acceptable.

3. ROI ANALYSIS:

	Budget	Actual
(a) Asset turnover	2.0	1.5
(b) Profit margin	10%	12%
ROI (a x b)	20%	18%

STUDY PLAN

1. Review the learning objectives, exhibits, and key terms for this chapter.

2. There is a template for Problem 13-21. Remember, the total income for the company should be the same regardless of the transfer price.

3. There is a template for Problem 13-22. This problem highlights the impact of allocating common costs. Note how the ranking changes using different allocation bases.

4. There is a template for Problem 13-31. This problem will help you understand the transfer price rule when the company is at full capacity and when it is below capacity.

5. There is a template for Problem 13-34. This problem will challenge you to find the most profitable volume for the company.

Chapter 14

Incentive Issues

This chapter discusses issues in the design and use of management performance evaluation and incentive plans. These plans should motivate managers to act in the organization's best interests. Good performance evaluation and incentive plans include "win-win" results such that managers are motivated to behave in ways that are mutually beneficial to their organizations and to themselves.

LEARNING OBJECTIVES

LO1   Describe key characteristics of divisional incentive compensation plans.

LO2   Know how incentive plans can affect the development phase of the product life cycle.

LO3   Know how the concept of economic value added affects management incentive systems.

LO4   Explain what constitutes fraudulent financial reporting.

LO5   Define the two most common types of fraud and demonstrate their impact on financial statements.

LO6   Recognize the incentives for committing financial fraud.

LO7   Explain how environmental conditions influence fraudulent conduct.

LO8   Identify control that can be instituted to prevent financial fraud.

REVIEW OF KEY CONCEPTS

LO1   Describe key characteristics of divisional incentive compensation plans.

   A. Divisional incentive compensation plans usually have the following characteristics:
   1. Cash bonuses and profit sharing plans reward managers for short-term performance.
   2. Deferred compensation, such as stock and stock options, is available to managers several years after they earn the compensation. Deferring receipt of proceeds from stock gives managers incentives to take actions that increase long-run share value.
   3. Firms give special awards for particular actions or extraordinary performance.

LO2   Know how incentive plans can affect the development phase of the product life cycle.

   A. A product's life cycle has four stages:
   1. Design and development: low sales volume; high costs for research, design, and development.
   2. Growth: sales increase.
   3. Maturity: profits decline due to high competition.
   4. Decline: market for product contracts.

   B. One of the major problems with short-run incentive plans is that managers are penalized in the current period for developing products that might produce long-run benefits. That is because accountants have traditionally written off the costs of developing new products as overhead. Managers who invest little in new-product development may thus appear to have more efficient performance in the short-run.

LO3   Know how the concept of economic value added affects management incentive systems.

   A. **Economic value added** (EVA) is the value created by a company in excess of the cost of capital for the investment base. Economic value added indicates how much shareholder wealth is created by company managers.

B. If a project's economic value added is negative, then shareholder wealth is being reduced and management should consider how to improve economic value added. Improving economic value added can be accomplished in three ways:
1. Increase profit without using more capital (cost cutting, for example).
2. Use less capital (use less equipment, for example).
3. Invest capital in high-return projects.

Test Your Understanding

Question: Assume a company invested $20 million of capital in a particular produce line. If the company's cost of capital is 10%, how much must the product line return in order to add economic value to the company?

Answer: The project must return more than $2,000,000.

LO4   Explain what constitutes fraudulent financial reporting.

A. **Fraudulent financial reporting** is intentional conduct resulting in materially misleading financial statements.

B. For financial reporting to be fraudulent:
1. It must result from intentional or reckless conduct, and
2. The resulting misstatements must be material to the financial statements.

C. To be **material**, the misstatement must be large enough to affect the judgment of a responsible person relying on the information.

LO5   Define the two most common types of fraud and demonstrate their impact on financial statements.

A. Employees at all levels in the organization, from top management to low-level employees, might participate in fraudulent financial reporting.

B. The two most common types of fraud involve improper revenue recognition and overstating inventory.

LO6   Recognize the incentives for committing financial fraud.

Managers given a short-term perspective by their employment (promotions) and pay (bonuses) arrangements will have an incentive to "manage earnings'.

LO7 Explain how environmental conditions influence fraudulent conduct.

    A. The Treadway Commission, in 1987, concluded that fraudulent financial reporting occurs because of a combination of pressures, incentives, opportunities, and environment.

    B. The Commission listed examples of pressures to perform that may lead to financial fraud, including, unrealistic budget pressures, and emphasis on short-term performance.

    C. The tone from the top most strongly influences fraudulent financial reporting.

LO8 Identify control that can be instituted to prevent financial fraud.

    A. **Internal controls** are policies and procedures designed to provide top management with reasonable assurances that actions undertaken by employees will meet organizational goals.

    B. A fundamental principle of internal control to prevent fraud is **separation of duties**. Thus, one person does not carry out a series of tasks that could result in a fraud.

    C. **Collusion** is the cooperative effort of employees to commit fraud or other unethical acts.

    D. Internal auditor help management or the board of directors. They can deter fraud by reviewing and testing internal controls and ensuring controls are in place and working well.

    E. Independent auditors express an opinion on published financial statements. They review the company's internal controls to help reduce fraud.

    F. Incentive problems in the international market.
        1. There are many cultural differences between countries that affect business practices.
        2. In 1977, the Foreign Corrupt Practices Act (FCPA) makes it illegal for any U.S. citizen or company to bribe or make gifts to foreign government officials in the course of business.

KEY TERMS

LO3 Know how the concept of economic value added affects management incentive systems.

Economic Value Added (EVA)	Annual after-tax operating profit minus the total annual cost of capital

LO4 Explain what constitutes fraudulent financial reporting.

Fraudulent financial reporting	Intentional or reckless conduct that results in materially misleading financial statements.

LO8 Identify controls that can be instituted to prevent financial fraud.

Internal controls	Policies and procedures designed to provide management with reasonable assurance that employees behave in a way that enables the firm to meet its organizational goals.
Collusion	Cooperative effort by employees to commit fraud or other unethical acts.

SELF-TEST

LO3   ECONOMIC VALUE ADDED:

Assume a company has the following facts for a project implemented during the current period:

Capital Employed:	
Equipment	$1,000,000
Land	750,000
Building	2,000,000
Total Capital Employed	$3,750,000

The project is expected to generate an after-tax operating profit of $600,000. To finance the project, the company will use both new debt and additional equity as follows:

Debt	$1,750,000
Equity	2,000,000

The interest rate on the debt is 10%. Equity holders expect a 15% return.

Calculate the economic value added by this project.

LO4   2. FRAUDULENT FINANCIAL INFORMATION:

The New York Times reported that Empire Blue Cross and Blue Shield said the results of an internal inquiry showed the company filed false information with the New York State Insurance Department for years. The management of the company made an official announcement that it had been keeping double records and understating its losses. The inaccurate figures were used to influence legislation overhauling the state's insurance industry.

During the four years, Empire Blue Cross and Blue Shield admitted to filing inaccurate reports, it lobbied heavily, and successfully, for a change in the state law that forced its competitors to accept some of the high-risk customers that only Empire had previously been required to take.

REQUIRED:

a.   Why did management misstate the accounting losses on the high-risk customers?

b.   What might be some reasons the management of the company felt pressured into misstating financial information?

c.   Is this an example of fraudulent financial reporting?

LO7   3. THE TREADWAY COMMISSION:

The 1987 recommendations of the Treadway Commission focused on publicly held companies. For each area listed below, explain how a company can improve its overall financial reporting process and increase the likelihood of preventing fraudulent financial reporting and detect it earlier when it occurs.

a. Tone at the Top

b. Internal Accounting and Audit Function

SOLUTIONS

---

1. <u>ECONOMIC VALUE ADDED</u> :

Capital Employed:

Equipment	$1,000,000
Land	750,000
Building	2,000,000
Total Capital Employed	$3,750,000

After-Tax Operating Profit		$600,000
Cost of Capital:		
Debt ($1,750,000 at 10%)	$175,000	
Equity ($2,000,000 at 15%)	300,000	
Total cost of capital		$475,000
Economic value added		$125,000

2. FRAUDULENT FINANCIAL REPORTING:

    a. Empire Blue Cross and Blue Shield showed higher losses on certain high-risk policyholders in order to influence legislation. If the company could charge higher prices for this group, or shift the policies to another insurance company, it would show more profits.

    b. Perhaps Empire Blue Cross and Blue Shield managers felt they would have more job security if the company looked better financially. Also, If the company had a profit incentive system, managers may have been motivated to improve reported profits.

    c. Yes. To be considered fraudulent financial reporting, the conduct must be intentional or reckless and the misstatement must be material to the financial statements. Both conditions appear to have been met.

3. THE TREADWAY COMMISSION:

    a. The tone set by top management influences the corporate environment within which financial reporting occurs. To set the right tone, top management must identify and assess the factors that could lead to fraudulent financial reporting. In addition, top management must be good role models.

    b. The internal audit function must be designed to fulfill the financial reporting responsibilities the corporation has undertaken as a public company. All public companies must have an effective and objective internal audit function. The internal auditor's qualifications, staff, status within the company, reporting lines, and relationship with the audit committee of the board of directors must be adequate to ensure the internal audit function's effectiveness and objectivity.

STUDY PLAN

1. Review the learning objectives, exhibits, and key terms for this chapter.

2. Review the organization chart in Chapter 1 of the text . Why does the internal audit function have the ability to communicate directly to the Board of Directors?

3. In addition to the financial fraud described in exercise 2, the text presents a summary of recent cases reported in the newspapers. You might be interested in reading in the text about Leslie Fay (Problem 27) and H.J. Heinz Company (Problem 28).

4. There are templates for Problems 14-19, 14-24, and 14-30.

Chapter 15

———◆———

Managerial Accounting Systems in Alternative Production Settings

This chapter shows how the accounting system records and reports the flow of costs in organizations. This chapter provides an overview of the ways different types of organization account for their production costs.

LEARNING OBJECTIVES

LO1   Explain the need for recording costs by department and assigning costs to products.

LO2   Understand how the Work-in-Process account describes the transformation of inputs into outputs in a company and accounts for the costs incurred in the process.

LO3   Compare and contrast normal costing and actual costing.

LO4   Know various production methods and the different accounting systems each requires.

LO5   Compare and contrast job costing and process systems.

LO6   Compare and contrast product costing in service organizations and that in manufacturing companies.

LO7   Identify ethical issues in job costing.

LO8   Recognize components of just-in-time (JIT) production methods and understand
        how accountants adapt costing systems to them.
LO9   Know how to compute end-of-period inventory value using equivalent units of
        production (Appendix in the text)

TEXTBOOK EXHIBITS

Exhibit 15.1 shows the relation between departmental and product costing.
Exhibit 15.2 shows each department has a separate Work-in-Process account.
Exhibit 15.3 provides a comparison of various production methods and their accounting
systems.
Exhibit 15.4 depicts the flow of costs in a service organization. Note the organization uses
job costing.
Exhibit 15.5 presents an income statement for a service organization.
Exhibit 15.6 compares backflush costing with traditional sequential tracking of costs. Note
the substantial reduction of transactions that must be recorded when the company uses
backflush costing.
Exhibit 15.7 presents just-in-time cost flows.

REVIEW OF KEY CONCEPTS

LO1   Explain the need for recording costs by department and assigning costs to products.

    A.   For purposes of planning and performance evaluation, accountants record
              costs by department or other responsibility centers.

    B.   In recording costs by department, the accounting system has served its
              function of providing data for departmental performance evaluation.

    C.   The accounting system records the costs of direct materials, direct labor,
              and manufacturing overhead incurred in production in separate accounts
              for the various departments.

LO2   Understand how the Work-in-Process account both describes the transformation of
        inputs into outputs in a company and accounts for the costs incurred in the process.

    A.   The Work-in-Process is the account that both **describes** the transformation
              of inputs into outputs and **accounts for** the costs incurred in the process.

    B.   In most companies, each department records its costs. Thus, each
              department has a separate Work-in-Process accounting.

C.   The basic cost flow equation is:

Beginning Balance + Transfers In = Transfers Out + Ending Balance
or, in symbols,

$$BB + TI = TO + EB$$

D.   Transfers in to the work in process represents the material, labor, and overhead used in production.

LO3   Compare and contrast normal costing and actual costing.

A.   **Actual unit costs** reflect the traditional historic cost recorded in the financial accounting records and include actual direct materials, actual direct labor, and actual manufacturing overhead per unit. If manufacturing costs are accumulated during interim periods, it is possible for actual manufacturing overhead per unit to be substantially different from quarter to quarter or month to month.

B.   **Normal unit costs** incorporate a constant amount of the overhead to each unit produced throughout the year. To calculate the normal amount of overhead that should be assigned to every unit produced, a predetermined overhead rate is used.

C   The **predetermined overhead rate** is calculated at the beginning of the annual period by dividing the estimated manufacturing overhead for the entire year by the expected output for the year. As units are produced, the normal overhead rate per unit is added to the actual direct material and actual direct labor costs to compute the total cost of the unit. Normal costing assures the same per unit overhead throughout the year, regardless of month to month fluctuations in actual costs and activity levels.

D.   Overhead rates can be calculated using many different cost drivers or allocation bases. Managers would choose the cost drive or base that best correlates overhead costs with the cost object.

E.   A **cost driver** is a factor that causes an activity's cost. For example, machine hours could be the factor that causes energy and maintenance costs for a machine.

F.	Overhead costs are applied to production using four steps:
1.	Select a cost driver or allocation base.
2.	Estimate the amount of overhead and the level of activity for the period.
3.	Compute the predetermined overhead rate.
4.	Apply overhead to production.

Test Your Understanding

Question: When does a company calculate its predetermined overhead rate?

Answer: At the beginning of the period, using estimated amounts for the numerator and the denominator.

LO4	Know various production methods and the different accounting systems each requires.

A.	Production methods vary across organizations, depending on the type of product. Some companies produce jobs, others produce products in a continuous flow process.

B.	Companies that produce jobs include print shops, custom construction, and defense contractors. These companies all produce customized products which are called jobs. Companies producing customized products use job costing to record the cost of their products. Many service organizations also use job costing.

C.	Continuous flow processing is at the opposite end of the continuum from job shops. Companies using continuous flow processing mass-produce homogeneous products in a continuous flow. Chemical processing companies and cereal producers are examples of companies that would use process costing to account for the cost of their products.

D.	Many companies use a hybrid of job and process costing, called operation costing. Operations are standardized methods of making a product that are performed repeatedly in production methods, like process costing. Materials can be different for each product or batch of products like job costing. Car manufacturers that offer a variety of models use operations costing.

LO5   Compare and contrast job costing and process systems.

A.   In job costing, firms collect costs for each "unit" produced. Often each department collects costs for evaluating the performance of departmental personnel.

B.   In process costing, firms accumulate costs in a department or production process during an accounting period, then spread those costs evenly over the unit produced that period, computing an average cost. Unit costs are derived by using the following formula:

Unit cost = <u>Total Manufacturing Cost Incurred During the Period</u>
Total Units Produced During the Period

C.   Process costing does not require as much record keeping as job costing because it does not require keeping track of the cost of each job. However, process costing only informs decision makers about the average cost of the units, not the cost of each particular unit or job.

D.   Cost-benefit analysis provides the answer why firms prefer one accounting system to another. Management and accountants must examine the costs and benefits of information and pick the method that best fits the organization's production operations.

Test Your Understanding

Question: If a company's nature of production is described as heterogeneous units and each unit is large, would the firm likely use job costing or process costing?

Answer: Job costing. Process costing is usually used for firms whose production process involves homogeneous units, continuous process, and many small units.

LO6   Compare and contrast product costing in service organization and that in manufacturing companies.

A.   Service organizations, like manufacturing companies, need good managerial accounting information. Service organizations must be especially sensitive to the timeliness and the quality of the service they provide to their customers.

B.   The flow of costs in a service organization is similar to that in manufacturing. The service provided requires labor and overhead. Service organizations often collect costs by departments for performance evaluation.

C. Service organizations often use job costing to determine the cost of jobs.

LO7 Identify ethical issues in job costing.

A. Improprieties in job costing generally are caused by one or more of the following actions:
1. Misstating the stage of completion of jobs.
2. Charging costs to the wrong job or categories.
3. Misrepresenting the costs of jobs.

B. To avoid the appearance of cost overruns on jobs, job supervisors sometimes ask employees to charge costs to the wrong job. This practice misleads managers who rely on accurate cost information for pricing, cost control, and other decisions. It also leads to unfair selling prices if the job is on a cost plus fee basis.

LO8 Recognize components of just-in-time (JIT) production methods and understand how accountants adapt costing systems to them.

A. Many companies have adopted just-in-time methods for parts of their production. Management uses just-in-time methods to obtain materials just in time for production and to provide finished goods just in time for sale.

B. This practice reduces, or potentially eliminates, inventories and the cost of carrying them.

C. In addition, just-in-time requires that workers immediately correct the process making defective units because they have no inventory where they can hide defective units. Eliminating inventories exposes production problems and requires workers to immediately correct them.

D. Companies that use JIT production methods can realize significant savings in staff time and costs to compute ending inventory values. Companies record costs directly in Cost of Goods Sold, using a method called **backflush costing,** to transfer any costs back to the inventory accounts.

E. JIT production began in Japan, but is now found in companies throughout the world.

KEY TERMS

LO2 Understand how the Work-in-Process account both describes the transformation of inputs into outputs in a company and accounts for the costs incurred in the process.

Cost flow equation	Beginning Balance + Transfer in = Transfers Out + Ending Balance; BB + TI = TO + EB

LO3 Compare and contrast normal costing and actual costing.

Normal costing	Method of allocating costs to products using actual direct materials, actual direct labor, and predetermined factory overhead rates.
Predetermined overhead rate	Rate used in applying overhead to products or departments and developed at the start of a period by dividing the estimated overhead cost by the estimated number of units of the overhead allocation base.
Cost driver	A factor that causes an activity's costs.
Allocation base	A cost driver used for applying overhead to production.

LO4 Know various production methods and the different accounting systems each requires.

Job	A customized product.
Job costing	Accumulation of costs for a particular identifiable product, known as a job, as it moves through production.
Continuous flow processing	Mass production of homogeneous

products in a continuous flow.

Operations

Standardized methods of making a product that are performed repeatedly in production of identifiable batches of products. Materials can be different for each product or batch of products like job costing.

Operations costing

A costing system that uses job costing to assign material costs and process costing to assign conversion costs.

Process costing

A method of cost accounting based on average costs (total cost divided by the equivalent units of work done in a period). Typically used for assembly lines or for products that are produced in a series of steps that are more continuous than discrete.

LO8 Recognize components of just-in-time (JIT) production methods and understand how accountants adapt costing systems to them.

Just-in-time (JIT) method

System of managing inventory for manufacturing in which a firm purchases or manufactures each component just before the firm uses it. JIT systems have much smaller, ideally no, carrying costs for inventory.

Backflush costing

A method that works backward from the output to assign manufacturing costs to work-in-process inventories.

SELF-TEST

LO3   1.   DIFFERENCES BETWEEN ACTUAL AND NORMAL COSTING:

The Hardnose Company uses direct labor hours as the cost driver for deriving a predetermined overhead rate. At the beginning of the year the company estimated the following manufacturing costs:

Estimated direct material (2 units of A @ $ .60)	$1.20	per unit
Estimated direct labor (2 hours @ $4.00 per hour)	$8.00	per unit
Estimated variable overhead (2 hrs @ $2.50 per hour)	$5.00	per unit
Estimated fixed overhead (total annual cost)	$21,000	
Estimated total annual production	10,000	units

At the end of the year, the company's records reflected the following actual results:

Actual direct material (2 units of A @ $ .65)	$1.30	per unit
Actual direct labor (3 hours @ $4.00 per hour)	$12.00	per unit
Actual variable overhead (3 hours @ $3.00 per hour)	$9.00	per unit
Actual fixed overhead (total annual cost)	$24,000	
Actual total annual production	10,000	units

REQUIRED:

a.   What is the actual fixed overhead rate per unit?

b.   What is the actual per unit using actual costing?

c.   What is the predetermined overhead rate per direct labor hour?

d.   How much overhead is applied to each unit?

e   What is the cost per unit using normal costing?

LO2   2. USING THE ACCOUNTING EQUATION

Assume the following facts:

Beginning materials inventory	$30
Beginning work-in-process inventory	26
Beginning finished goods inventory	50
Direct materials requisitioned	80
Direct labor	35
Manufacturing overhead	
(including $2 of indirect materials)	16
Ending materials inventory	34
Ending work-in-process inventory	23
Ending finished goods inventory	55

REQUIRED:

a. Determine the amount of materials purchased during the period.

b. Determine the cost of goods manufactured during the period.

c. Determine the cost of goods sold during the period.

LO4   3. JOB COSTING FOR A MANUFACTURING COMPANY

The Wisher Products Company uses a job costing system. The company estimated its annual overhead to be $50,000, and the number of direct labor hours for the year to be 10,000 hours. In the first month, the following jobs were completed:

	Job #1	Job #2
Direct materials used	$1,000	$1,500
Direct labor cost	$2,000	$2,500
Direct labor hours	1,000 hours	1,200 hours

REQUIRED:

a. What is the company's predetermined overhead rate using direct labor hours as the base?

b. What is the overhead assigned to job #1?

c. What is the overhead assigned to job #2?

d. What is the total manufacturing cost of job #1?

e. What is the total manufacturing cost of job #2?

LO4   4. PROCESS COSTING:

Assume the company in Exercise 3 used a process system. The following costs were accumulated by departments:

	Dept. A	Dept. B
Direct materials used	$2,000	$ 500
Direct labor cost	$3,000	$1,500
Direct labor hours	1,500 hours	700 hours

REQUIRED:

a.   What is the company's predetermined overhead rate?

b.   What are the overhead costs charged to Dept. A?

c.   What are the total costs accumulated in Dept. A?

d.   What are the overhead costs charged to Dept. B?

e.   What are the total costs accumulated in Dept. B?

f.   What are the unit costs associated with the two jobs?

SOLUTIONS

1   .DIFFERENCES BETWEEN ACTUAL AND NORMAL COSTING:

   a.   First compute total hours expected: 10,000 units x 3 hours each = 30,000 hours.
        Then, $24,000/30,000 hours = $ .80/hour or $2.40/unit

   b. $1.30 + $12.00 + $9.00 + $2.40 = $24.70/unit

   c.   First compute total direct labor hours expected: 10,000 units x 2 hrs. each = 20,000 hrs
        Then, $21,000/20,000 hour = $1.05/hour

   d.   Variable overhead applied is $7.50 (3 hrs. x $2.50/hr.)
        Fixed overhead applied is $3.15 (3 hrs. x $1.05/hr.)
        Total overhead applied is $10.65.

   e. $1.30 + $12.00 + $7.50 + $3.15 = $23.95/unit

2.   USING THE ACCOUNTING EQUATION:

   a. $86 determined by solving for X: [30 + X - (80 + 2) = 34] where 2 represents indirect
        materials.

   b. $134 determined by (26 + 80 + 35 + 16 - 23)

   c. $129 determined by (50 + 134 - 55)

3. JOB COSTING FOR A MANUFACTURING COMPANY:

   a. $50,000/10,000 hours = $5/direct labor hour

   b.   1,000 hours @ $5 per hour = $5,000

   c.   1,200 hours @ $5 per hour = $6,000

   d. $1,000 + $2,000 + $5,000 = $8,000

   e. $1,500 + $2,500 + $6,000 = $10,000

4. PROCESS COSTING:

a. $50,000/10,000$ hours $= \$5/$direct labor hour
   This is the same as Exercise 3 part a.

b. 1,500 hours @ $5 per hour = $7,500

c. $2,000 + $3,000 + $7,500 = $12,500

d. 700 hours @ $5 per hour = $3,500

e. $500 + $1,500 + $3,500 = $5,500

f. [Dept A. + Dept B.]/2 jobs = [$12,500 + $5,500]/2 = $9,000 per job

STUDY PLAN

1. Review the learning objectives, exhibits, and key terms for this chapter.

2. Review Exhibit 15.2 in the text. You should now understand the basic cost flow equation: TI + BB = TO + EB . It is used for determining materials used during the period, the cost of goods manufactured, and the cost of goods sold. Review the Self-Study problem 15.1. The text exercises 18 through 22 use these relationships.

3. Do Exercise 24 in the text. Note the company does not use a work-in-process account. All manufacturing costs are charged directly to the cost of goods sold account. The finished goods inventory account is charged only at the end of the period based on the cost of the ending inventory. This form of backflush accounting substantially reduces the number of entries needed to account for inventories.

4. There is a template for Problem 15-32 in the text. The problem applies overhead to a bank environment.

5. There is a template for Problem 15-34 in the text.

6. There is a template for Problem 15-35 in the text.

7. There is a template for Problem 15-38 in the text. This problem is a process cost problem using the information found in the appendix of the text.

Chapter 16

Cost Allocation

This chapter discusses concepts and methods of assigning indirect costs, like overhead, to departments. We call such cost assignments cost allocation.

LEARNING OBJECTIVES

LO1   Understand the nature of common (or indirect) costs.
LO2   Know why companies allocate common costs to departments and products.
LO3   Know how to allocate service department costs to product departments and product department costs to products.
LO4   Compare allocation of marketing and administrative costs to allocation of manufacturing costs.

TEXTBOOK EXHIBITS

Exhibit 16.1 shows an organization chart for a bank.
Exhibit 16.2 shows the steps in allocating costs.
Exhibit 16.3 demonstrates the step allocation method.
Exhibit 16.4 lists various allocation bases.

REVIEW OF KEY CONCEPTS

LO1   Understand the nature of common (or indirect) costs.

Accountants distinguish between a direct cost and an indirect cost. A **direct cost** can be identified specifically with, or traced directly to a cost object. It needs no allocation. A common or **indirect cost** results from the joint use of a facility by several products, departments, or processes. It must be allocated to a cost object.

LO2   Know why companies allocate common costs to departments and products

Firms must allocate common costs to develop product cost information for the purpose of pricing and bidding, contract cost reimbursement, motivation, asset valuation, and income determination.

LO3   Know how to allocate service department costs to product departments and product department costs to products

A.   First, allocate overhead costs that are directly attributable to a service or product department. Then allocate other overhead costs based on some cost driver. The two methods used to allocate service department costs to product departments are the step method and the reciprocal method. Next allocate product department costs to products based on some cost driver.

B.   The **step method** is often used to allocate costs from service departments to product departments. This procedure starts by allocating one service department's costs to product departments and to all other service departments; then a second service department's costs are allocated to product departments and all other service departments except the first one. Mathematically, the result will differ depending on the order of the allocation. Usually we begin with the service department that received the smallest dollar mount of service from the other service departments.

C.   A more complex alternative is the **reciprocal method** which recognizes service departments use each others services.

D.   The direct method allocates service department costs to product departments directly. No service department cost is allocated to any other service department.

Copyright ©1997 Harcourt Brace & Company

Test Your Understanding

Question: A company has two service departments and two product departments, as follows:

	Costs	Labor Hours		Costs	Labor Hours
Service Department A:	$100	300	Product Department 1:	$500	1,000
Service Department B:	$300	200	Product Department 2:	$750	4,000

Using the direct method, how much of the service departments costs are allocated to each of the product departments?

Answer: Service Department A is allocated 20% to Product Department 1, or $20; and 80% to Product Department 2, or $80; Service Department B is also allocated 20% to Product Department 1, or $60; and 80% to Product Department 2, or $240. The direct method allocates service department costs directly to product departments.

LO4   Compare allocation of marketing and administrative costs to allocation of manufacturing costs

Marketing and administrative expenses are allocated using similar techniques as those used in manufacturing cost analysis.

KEY TERMS

LO1   Understand the nature of common (or indirect) costs.

Direct cost	Cost of direct material and direct labor incurred in producing a product.
Indirect or common cost	Cost resulting from the use of raw materials, a facility, or a service that benefits several products or departments and that a firm must allocate to those products or departments.

LO3   Know how to allocate service department costs to product departments and product department costs to products.

Service department cost allocation   Allocation of service department costs to product departments.

Service department   A department that provides services to other departments, rather than directly work on a salable product.

Allocation base   Accounting often assigns common costs to cost objectives with some systematic method. The allocation base specifies the method.

Step method   The method for allocating service department costs that starts by allocating one service department's cost to a product department and to all other service department. Then the firm allocates a second service department's cost to production departments and all other service departments except the first one. And so on.

Direct method   The methods for allocating service department costs that allocates directly to producing departments.

SELF-TEST

LO3 1. ALLOCATING SERVICE DEPARTMENT COSTS: USING THE DIRECT METHOD:

(This exercise uses the same information as exercise 14 in the text, but demonstrates the use of the direct method. The direct method allocates service department costs directly to production departments. None of the service department costs are assigned to the other service departments.

General Factory Administration and Maintenance are service departments in the Newington Box Company. Management has decided to allocate maintenance costs on the basis of the area in each department and general factory administration costs on the basis of labor hours the employees worked in each of their respective departments.

The following data appears in the company records for the current period:

	General Factory Admin.	Maintenance	Cutting	Assembly
Area Occupied (square feet)	1,000	0	1,000	3,000
Labor Hours		100	100	400
Direct Labor Costs			$1,500	$4,000
Service Dept. Costs			$1,200	$2,400

REQUIRED:

a. Use the direct method to allocate service department costs to the operating departments. (Note: The direct method allocates service department costs directly to product departments. None of the service department costs are allocated to the other service departments.)

b. Use the step method to allocate service department costs to the operating departments, starting with general factory administration.

c. What are the total service department costs allocated using each method?

LO3   2.   USING MULTIPLE COST DRIVERS TO ALLOCATE COSTS:

Plum Company produced 3,050 crates of product this year. Assume the Plum Manufacturing Company uses three allocation bases to allocate overhead costs from departments to job: number of inspections, number of job setup hours, and number of machine hours worked. The information needed to compute the allocation rates follows:

	Grinding Dept.		Packing Dept	
		Units of		Units of
	Costs	Activity	Costs	Activity
1. No. of inspections	$3,000	150	$5,000	250
2. No. of job setup hours	$8,000	200	$7,500	150
3. No. of machine hours	$6,000	1,200	$1,000	50

Job number AX4056 contained 20 crates and required the following activities:

Grinding Dept.: 3 inspections, 10 setup hours, 24 machine hours
Packing Dept.:   4 inspections, 2 setup hours, 5 machine hours

REQUIRED:

a.   Allocate overhead cost to Job number AX4056 using the multiple cost drivers.

b.   Management believes the multiple cost drivers are too time consuming and wants to change to one cost driver. They selected number of crates as the cost driver. Allocate the overhead cost to Job number AX4056 using number of crates as the denominator activity.

c.   Why are multiple cost drivers useful to managers?

SOLUTIONS

1. ALLOCATING SERVICE DEPARTMENT COSTS: USING THE DIRECT METHOD:

   a. Direct method

G.F.A.	Maintenance	Cutting	Assembly
	(2,400)	(1/4) 600	(3/4)1,800
(1,200)		(1/5) 240	(4/5) 960
Total allocated		$840	$2,760

   b. Step method, starting with General Factory Administration

G.F.A.	Maintenance	Cutting	Assembly
$1,200	2,400	N/A	N/A
(1,200)	(1/6)200	(1/6)200	(4/6)800
$0	$2,600		
	(2,600)	(1/4)650	(3/4)1,950
	$0	$850	$2,750

   c. Using the direct method, a total of $3,600 ($840 + $2,760) is allocated.
      Using the step method, a total of $3,600 ($840 + $2,760) is also allocated.

2. USING MULTIPLE COST DRIVERS TO ALLOCATE COSTS:

a.   Assigning overhead costs using multiple cost drivers:

Overhead rates	Grinding	Packing
1. No. of inspections	$3,000/150 = $20	$5,000/250 = $20
2. No. of job setups	$8,000/200 = $40	$7,500/150 = $50
3. No. of machine hours	$6,000/1,200 = $5	$1,000/50 = $20

In step 2, assign cost driver rates to product:

Grinding Dept. :
Inspection	$20 x 3 =	$60
Job setups	$40 x 10 =	400
Machine hours	$5 x 24 =	120
Total overhead in Grinding Dept.		$580

Packing Dept.:
Inspection	$20 x 4 =	$80
Job setups	$50 x 2 =	100
Machine hours	$20 x 5 =	100
Total overhead in Packing Dept.		$280

Total overhead assigned to Job AX4056 $860

b. Using number of crates as the cost driver, the overhead rate would be:

Total inspection costs	$8,000	
Total job setup costs	15,500	
Total machine hour costs	7,000	
Total overhead costs		$30,500
Total number of crates		3,050
Overhead cost/crate		$10

Since Job AX4056 contained 20 crates, the total overhead assigned would be $200 ($10 x 20).

c. Multiple cost drivers provides a more detailed understanding about the activities that drives the cost of the product. If management used the single cost driver, the product cost would not reflect that this product required a more than the average amount of inspection cost, job setup cost and machine cost. Traditional cost allocation procedures assigns the same amount of overhead cost to each crate. It appears resources are consumed disproportionately for this job. If multiple cost drivers were used, each crate would be assigned $43 ($860/20) of overhead rather than the average cost per crate of $10 .

Management may, for example, try to reduce setup time in order to reduce the cost of the product. Multiple cost drivers would provide more accurate information concerning the impact of reducing setup time on the cost of the product. Alternatively, management may want price this product to more fairly reflect the resources consumed by the costly inspections, setup hours and machine hours.

STUDY PLAN

1. Review the learning objectives, exhibits, and key terms in this chapter.

2. The study guide Exercise 14 is similar to Exercise 16 in the text. When you complete Exercise 14 you should confirm that all methods allocate a total of $3,600 to the producing departments. However, each method results in a different amount allocated to each department and the departmental overhead rates will differ under each alternative method. Even within the step method, the results will vary depending on which service department you allocate first!

3. There is a template for Problem 16-16. This problem allocates service departments directly to operating departments.

4. There is a template for Problem 16-17. This problem is an extension of problem 16-16 and allocates service departments using the step method.

5. There is a template for Problem 16-19. This problem demonstrates how to perform cost allocations in a retail setting.

6. There is a template for Problem 16-21. This problem requires both the step and direct methods.

Chapter 17

◆

Introduction to Financial Statement Analysis

This chapter introduced tools and techniques for analyzing financial statements. Most financial statement analysis attempts to assess the profitability and risk of a firm. The analyst accomplishes this objective by examining relations between various financial statement items, expressed in the form of financial statement ratios. This chapter describes several commonly used financial statement ratios and illustrates their usefulness in assessing a firm's profitability and risk.

LEARNING OBJECTIVES

LO1   Understand the relation between the expected return and risk of investment alternatives and the role financial statement analysis can play in providing information about returns and risk.

LO2   Understand the usefulness of the rate of return on assets (ROA) as a measure of a firm's operating profitability independent of financing and the insights gained by disaggregating ROA into profit-margin and assets-turnover components.

LO3   Understand the usefulness of the rate of return on common stockholders' equity (ROCE) as a measure of profitability that incorporates a firm's particular mix of financing and the insights gained by disaggregating ROCE into profit-margin, assets-turnover, and leverage ratio components.

LO4 Understand the strengths and weaknesses of earnings per common share as a measure of profitability.

LO5 Understand the distinction between short-term liquidity risk and long-term liquidity (solvency) risk and the financial statement ratios used to assess these two dimensions of risk.

LO6 Develop skills to interpret effectively the results of an analysis of profitability and risk.

LO7 Develop skills to prepare proforma financial statements (Appendix 17.1 in the text).

LO8 Understand the usefulness of pro forma financial statements in the valuation of a firm (Appendix 17.1 in the text).

TEXTBOOK EXHIBITS

Exhibit 17-1 shows the relation between financial statement analysis and investment decisions.

Exhibit 17-2 presents comparative income statements for the Horrigan Corporation.

Exhibit 17-3 presents comparative balance sheets for the Horrigan Corporation.

Exhibit 17-4 presents comparative statements of cash flows for the Horrigan Corporation.

Exhibit 17-5 displays the disaggregation of the rate of return on assets into the profit margin and asset turnover.

Exhibit 17-6 presents common size income statements for the Horrigan Company.

Exhibit 17-7 calculates asset turnover ratios.

Exhibit 17-8 calculates profitability ratios for the Abbott Corporation.

Exhibit 17-9 graphically represents the rates of return for the Horrigan Corporation.

Exhibit 17-10 demonstrates the effects of financial leverage on the rate of return on common shareholders' equity.

Exhibit 17-11 disaggregates the rate of return on common shareholders' equity for the Horrigan Corporation.

Exhibit 17-12 shows three levels of profitability ratios.

Exhibit 17-13 shows the two forms of the debt ratio for the Horrigan Corporation.

Exhibit 17-14 summarizes the calculation of the financial statement ratios discussed in the chapter.

REVIEW OF KEY CONCEPTS

LO1 Understand the relation between the expected return and risk of investment alternatives and the role financial statement analysis can play in providing information about returns and risk.

A. The first question the analyst asks in analyzing a set of financial statements is, "What do I look for?' The answer includes the return you anticipate from an investment and the risk associated with that return.

B. **Return** is the increase in wealth from an investment. Investments in common stock yield their return in the form of dividends and changes in market prices. Investment in debt securities yield their return in the form of interest and changes in market prices.

C. **Risk** is a measure of the variability of the return on an investment. For a given expected amount of return, most people prefer less risk to more risk.

LO2 Understand the usefulness of the rate of return on assets (ROA) as a measure of a firm's operating profitability independent of financing and the insights gained by disaggregating ROA into profit-margin and assets-turnover components.

A. The **rate of return on assets (ROA)** measures a firm's performance in using assets to generate earnings independent of the financing of those assets.

B. The rate of return on assets relates the results of operating performance to the investments of firm without regard to how the firm financed the acquisition of those investments. Thus, the ROA attempts to measure the success of a firm in creating and selling goods and services to customers, activities that fall primarily within the responsibility of production and marketing personnel. The rate of return on assets excludes consideration of the particular mix of financing used. The calculation of ROA is:

$$\text{ROA} = \frac{\text{Net income} + \text{Interest Expense Net of Income Tax Savings}}{\text{Average Total Assets}}$$

C.   To study changes in the rate of return on assets, the analyst can disaggregate ROA into the product of two other ratios.

ROA =   Profit Margin Ratio   X   Total Assets Turnover Ratio

$$\text{ROA} = \frac{\text{Net income + Interest Expense (Net of Income Tax Savings)}}{\text{Sales}} \quad X \quad \frac{\text{Sales}}{\text{Average Total Assets}}$$

D.   The **profit margin ratio** measures a firm's ability to control the level of expenses relative to sales. A **common size** income statement is a useful tool for observing changes in the profit margin percentage.

E.   The **total assets turnover ratio** measures a firm's ability to generate sales from a particular level of investment in assets.

F.   The total asset turnover ratio aggregates the effects of the turnover ratios for the individual assets components. The analyst calculates three separate asset turnover ratios: accounts receivable, inventory turnover, and plant asset turnover.

G.   The rate at which accounts receivable turn over indicates how quickly the firm collects cash. The **accounts receivable turnover ratio** is calculated as follows:

$$\text{Accounts Receivable Turnover} = \frac{\text{Net Sales on Account}}{\text{Average Accounts Receivable}}$$

H.   The **inventory turnover ratio** indicates how fast firms sell their inventory items. The inventory turnover is calculated as follows:

$$\text{Inventory turnover} = \frac{\text{Cost of Goods Sold}}{\text{Average Inventory}}$$

I.   The **plant asset turnover ratio** measures the relation between the investment in plant assets (property, plant, and equipment) and sales. The plant asset turnover ratio is calculated as follows:

$$\text{Plant Asset Turnover} = \frac{\text{Sales}}{\text{Average Plant Assets}}$$

LO3   Understand the usefulness of the **rate of return on common stockholders' equity (ROCE)** as a measure of profitability that incorporates a firm's particular mix of financing and the insights gained by disaggregating ROCE into profit-margin, assets-turnover, and leverage ratio components.

A.   The **rate of return on common shareholders; equity** measures a firm's performance in using financing assets to generate earnings and is of primary interest to common shareholders. The calculation of the rate of return on common shareholders' equity is as follows:

$$\text{ROCE} = \frac{\text{Net Income - Dividends on Preferred Stock}}{\text{Average Common Shareholders' Equity}}$$

B.   The rate of return on assets measures the profitability of a firm before any payments to the suppliers of capital. The rate of return on common shareholders' equity will exceed the rate of return on assets whenever the rate of return on assets exceeds the after-tax cost of debt (assuming the firm has no preferred stock outstanding).

C.   **Financial leverage** describes financing with debt and preferred stock to increase the potential return to the residual common shareholders' equity. As long as a firm earns a rate of return on assets that exceeds the rate it paid for the capital used to acquire those assets, the rate of return to common shareholders will increase.

D.   The rate of return on common shareholders' equity disaggregates into several components as follows:

Rate of Return on Common Shareholders' Equity		Profit Margin Ratio (after interest expense and preferred dividends)		Total Assets Turnover Ratio		Leverage Ratio
	=		X		X	

LO4 Understand the strengths and weaknesses of earnings per common share as a measure of profitability.

A. **Earnings per share of common stock** provides a third measure of profitability. Earnings per share is calculated as follows:

$$EPS = \frac{\text{Net Income - Preferred Stock Dividends Declared}}{\text{Weighted Average Number of Common Shares Outstanding During the Period}}$$

B. A firm with securities outstanding that holders can convert into or exchange for shares of common stock may report two earnings-per-share amounts: basic earnings per share and fully diluted earning per share. Dilution occurs when a firm has securities outstanding, that, if exchanged for common shares, would decrease basic earnings per share.

C. Two firms with the same earnings and earnings per share will not be equally profitable if one of the firms requires twice the amount of assets or capital to generate those earnings as does the other firm. Thus, in comparing firms, earnings-per-share amounts have limited use.

D. Financial analysts often compare earnings-per-share amounts with the market price of the stock. They usually express this comparison as a **price-earnings ratio**. The price-earnings ratio is calculated as follows:

$$P/E \text{ ratio} = \frac{\text{Market Price per Share}}{\text{Earnings per Share}}$$

LO5 Understand the distinction between short-term liquidity risk and long-term liquidity (solvency) risk and the financial statement ratios used to assess these two dimensions of risk.

A. Analysts deciding between investments must consider their comparative risks. Various factors affect the risk of business firms:

1. Economywide factors, such as increased inflation or interest rates, unemployment, or recessions.

2. Industrywide factors, such as increased competition, lack of availability of raw materials, changes in technology, or increased government regulatory actions.

3. Firm-specific factors, such as labor strikes, loss of facilities due to fire or other casualty, or poor health of key managerial personnel.

B. Analysts assessing risk generally focus on the relative liquidity of a firm. Cash and near-cash assets provide a firm with the resources needed to adapt to the various types of risk; that is, liquid resources provide a firm with financial flexibility.

C. There are four measures for assessing short-term liquidity risk: (1) the current ratio, (2) the quick ratio, (3) the operating cash flow to current liabilities ratio, and (4) working capital turnover ratios.

D. The **current ratio** indicates a firm's ability to meet its short-term obligations and is calculated as follows:

$$\text{Current Ratio} = \frac{\text{Current Assets}}{\text{Current Liabilities}}$$

E. The **quick ratio**, sometimes called the acid test ratio, is a variation of the current ratio. It is another measure of a firm's ability to meet its short-term obligations. the numerator includes only highly liquid assets. Thus, the analyst usually includes cash, marketable securities and receivables. However, the facts in each case will indicate whether the analyst should include receivables or exclude inventory. The quick ratio is calculated as follows:

$$\text{Quick Ratio} = \frac{\text{Highly Liquid Assets}}{\text{Current Liabilities}}$$

F. The current ratio and the quick ratio use amount at a specific point in time and may be unusually large or small at that particular point in time. **Cash flow from operations to current liabilities** captures cash flow for a period of time and is calculated as follows:

Cash Flow
from Operations = $\underline{\text{Cash Flows from Operations for the Period}}$
to Current   Current Liabilities
Liabilities

G.   **Working Capital Turnover Ratios** captures the operating cycle of the firm. The operating cycle includes (1) purchasing inventory on account from suppliers, (2) selling inventory on account to customers, (3) collecting amounts due from customers, and (4) paying amounts due to suppliers.

1.   The **number of days that a firm holds inventories** indicates the length of the period between the purchase and sale of inventory during each operating cycle. The number of days that a firm holds inventories is calculated as follows:

365 days/inventory turnover ratio

2.   The number of days that a firm's receivable remain outstanding indicates the length of the period between the sale of inventory and the collection of cash from customers during each operating cycle. The number of **days that a firm's receivables remain outstanding** is calculated as follows:

365/accounts receivable turnover ratio

3.   The number of days that a firm's accounts payable remain outstanding indicates the length of the period between the purchase of inventory on account and the payment of cash to suppliers during each operating cycle. The **accounts payable turnover ratio** is calculated as follows:

Accounts Payable Turnover Ratio = $\underline{\text{Purchases on Account}}$
                                   Average Accounts Payable

The number of **days that a firm's payables remain outstanding** is calculated as follows:

365/accounts payable turnover ratio

H. Analysts use measures of **long-term liquidity risk** to evaluate a firm's ability to meet interest and principal payments on long-term debt and similar obligation as they come due. A firm's ability to generate profits over several years provides the best protection against long-term liquidity risk. Analysts measure long-term liquidity risk with debt ratios, the cash flow from operations to total liabilities ratio, and the interest coverage ratio.

I. The debt ratio has several variation, but the **long-term debt ratio** commonly appears in financial analysis. It reports the firm's long-term capital that debt holders furnish. The ratio is calculated as follows:

$$\text{Debt Ratio} = \frac{\text{Total Long-term Debt}}{\text{Total Long-Term Debt + Total Shareholders' Equity}}$$

J. Another form of the debt ratio is the debt-equity ratio. The debt-equity ratio is calculated as follows:

$$\text{Debt-Equity Ratio} = \frac{\text{Total Liabilities}}{\text{Total Liabilities + Total Shareholders' Equity}}$$

K. The debt ratios do not consider the availability of liquid assets to cover various levels of debt. The cash flow from operations to total liabilities ratio overcomes this deficiency. The cash flow from operations to total liabilities ratio is calculated as follows:

$$\begin{matrix}\text{Cash Flow from Operations} \\ \text{to Total Liabilities}\end{matrix} = \frac{\text{Cash Flow from Operations}}{\text{Average Total Liabilities}}$$

L. The number of times that earnings cover interest charges also measures long-term liquidity risk. The interest coverage ratio is calculated as follows:

$$\text{Interest Coverage Ratio} = \frac{\text{Net income Before Interest and Income Taxes}}{\text{Interest Expense}}$$

M. The **interest coverage ratio** attempts to indicate the relative protection that operating profitability provides bondholders, permitting them to assess the probability of a firm's failing to meet required interest payments. If bond indentures require periodic repayments of principal on long-term liabilities, the denominator of the ratio might include such repayments. The ratio would then be called the **fixed charges coverage ratio.**

LO6   Develop skills to interpret effectively the results of an analysis of profitability and risk.

There are many limitations of ratio analysis. These include:

A.   Because ratios use financial statement data as inputs, the same factors that cause financial statement themselves to have shortcomings will affect the ratios computed from them.

B.   Changes in many ratios correlate with each other.

C.   When comparing the size of a ratio between periods for the same firm, one must recognize conditions that have changed between the periods being compared.

D.   When comparing ratios of a particular firm with those of similar firms, one must recognize difference between the firms (for example, use of different methods of accounting, differences in the method of operations, and types of financing).

E.   Financial statement ratios alone cannot provide direct indicators of good or poor management. Such ratios indicate areas that the analyst should investigate further.

A Summary of Important Ratios

Short-term Liquidity Ratios

Ratio	Formula
Current Ratio	$\dfrac{\text{Current Assets}}{\text{Current Liabilities}}$
Quick Ratio (Acid-Test Ratio)	$\dfrac{\text{Highly Liquid Assets (Cash, Marketable Securities, Receivables)}}{\text{Current Liabilities}}$
Cash Flow from Operations to Current Liabilities Ratio	$\dfrac{\text{Net Cash from Operations}}{\text{Average Current Liabilities}}$
Accounts Receivable Turnover Ratio	$\dfrac{\text{Net Credit Sales}}{\text{Average Accounts Receivable}}$
Days Accounts Receivable Outstanding	$\dfrac{\text{Number of Days in Period (365 for a year)}}{\text{Accounts Receivable Turnover}}$
Inventory Turnover Ratio	$\dfrac{\text{Cost of Goods Sold}}{\text{Average Inventory}}$
Days Inventories Held	$\dfrac{\text{Number of Days in Period (365 for a year)}}{\text{Inventory Turnover}}$
Accounts Payable Turnover Ratio	$\dfrac{\text{Purchases}}{\text{Average Accounts Payable}}$
Days Accounts Payable Outstanding	$\dfrac{\text{Number of Days in Period (365 for a year)}}{\text{Accounts Payable Turnover Ratio}}$

Long-term Liquidity Ratios

Ratio	Formula
Long-term Debt Ratio	$\dfrac{\text{Total Long-term Debt}}{\text{Total Long-term Debt + Shareholders' Equity}}$
Debt-Equity Ratio	$\dfrac{\text{Total Liabilities}}{\text{Total Liabilities + Shareholders' Equity}}$
Cash Flow from Operations to Total Liabilities Ratio	$\dfrac{\text{Cash Flow from Operations}}{\text{Average Total Liabilities}}$
Interest Coverage Ratio	$\dfrac{\text{Net Income Before Interest Expense and Income Taxes}}{\text{Interest expense}}$

Profitability ratios

Ratio	Formula
Rate of Return on Assets	$\dfrac{\text{Net income + Interest Expense (net of tax effects)}}{\text{Average Total Assets}}$
Profit Margin Ratio (before interest effects)	$\dfrac{\text{Net income + Interest Expense (net of tax effects)}}{\text{Sales}}$
Various Expense Ratios	$\dfrac{\text{Various Expenses}}{\text{Sales}}$
Total Assets Turnover Ratio	$\dfrac{\text{Sales}}{\text{Average Total Assets}}$
Accounts Receivable Turnover Ratio	$\dfrac{\text{Net Sales on Account}}{\text{Average Accounts Receivable}}$
Inventory Turnover Ratio	$\dfrac{\text{Cost of Goods Sold}}{\text{Average Inventory}}$
Plant Asset Turnover Ratio	$\dfrac{\text{Sales}}{\text{Average Plant Assets}}$
Rate of Return on Common Shareholders' Equity	$\dfrac{\text{Net Income - Preferred Stock Dividends}}{\text{Average Common Shareholders' Equity}}$
Profit Margin Ratio (after interest expense and preferred dividends)	$\dfrac{\text{Net Income - Preferred Stock Dividends}}{\text{Sales}}$
Leverage Ratio	$\dfrac{\text{Average Total Assets}}{^\circ \text{ Average Common Shareholders' Equity}}$
Earnings per Share of Stock	$\dfrac{\text{Net Income - Preferred Stock Dividends}}{\text{Weighted Average No. of Common Shares Outstanding}}$

KEY TERMS

LO1 Understand the relation between the expected return and risk of investment alternatives and the role financial statement analysis can play in providing information about returns and risk.

Return	The increase in wealth from an investment.
Risk	A measure of the variability of the return on an investment.

Time-series analysis	Analysis of financial statements of a given firm for several periods of time.
Cross-sectional analysis	Analysis of financial statements of a given firm for a single period of time.

LO2 Understand the usefulness of the rate of return on assets (ROA) as a measure of a firm's operating profitability independent of financing and the insights gained by disaggregating ROA into profit-margin and assets-turnover components.

Profitability	Analysis of a firm's ability to generate earnings from the use of capital.
Rate of Return on Assets (ROA)	A measure of operating profitability that excludes the effects of financing.
Profit margin ratio	A measure of the firm's ability to generate earnings from sales.
Total assets turnover ratio	A measure of the firm's ability to generate sales from a given level of assets.
Accounts receivable turnover ratio	A measure of the frequency during a period that a firm turns its accounts receivable into cash.
Inventory turnover ratio	A measure of the frequency during a period that a firm turns its inventory into sales.
Plant assets turnover ratio	A measure of the frequency during a period that a firm converts amounts invested in property, plant, and equipment into sales.

LO3 Understand the usefulness of the rate of return on common stockholders' equity (ROCE) as a measure of profitability that incorporates a firm's particular mix of financing and the insights gained by disaggregating ROCE into profit-margin, assets-turnover, and leverage ratio components.

Rate of return on shareholders' equity	A measure of performance that incorporates the effects of a firm's financing decisions.
Financial leverage	The use of lower cost debt and preferred stock to increase the return to the residual common shareholders.
Leverage ratio	The relative proportion of capital provided by common shareholders contrasted with that provided by creditors and preferred shareholders.
Basic earnings per share of common stock	A measure of profitability that relates net income allocable to the common shareholders to the weighted average number of shares of common stock outstanding during a period.
Fully diluted earnings per share	A measure of profitability that reflects the dilutive effects of convertible securities and stock options and warrants.

LO5 Understand the distinction between short-term liquidity risk and long-term liquidity (solvency) risk and the financial ratios used to assess these two dimensions of risk.

Short-term liquidity risk	The risk that a firm will not have enough cash in the short-term to pay its debts.
Current ratio	A measure of short-term liquidity risk that relates current assets to current liabilities.

Quick or acid test ratio	A measure of short-term liquidity risk that relates a firm's most liquid assets to current liabilities.
Cash flow from operations to current liabilities ratio	A measure of short-term liquidity risk that relates cash flow from operations to average current liabilities for a period.
Accounts payable turnover ratio	A measure of frequency during a period that a firm pays its accounts payable.
Long-term liquidity risk	The risk that a firm will not have enough cash in the long-term to pay its debts.
Long-term debt ratio	A measure of the long-term liquidity risk that relates long-term debt to the sum of long-term debt plus shareholders' equity.
Accounts receivable turnover ratio	A measure of the number of times accounts receivable are collected in a period.
Debt-equity ratio	A measure of long-term liquidity risk that relates total long-term debt to shareholders' equity.
Cash flow from operations to total liabilities ratio	A measure of long-term liquidity risk that relates cash flow from operations to average liabilities for a period.
Interest coverage ratio	A measure of long-term liquidity risk that relates net income before interest expense and income taxes to interest expense.
Fixed charges interest ratio	A measure of long-term liquidity risk similar to the interest coverage ratio but includes other fixed payments, such as for leases.

SELF-TEST

LO6   ANALYSIS OF FINANCIAL STATEMENTS:

Marooth Corporation
Income Statement
For Year Ended December 31, 1996

$ in millions	1996
Revenue	$329,000
Cost of sales	(200,000)
Gross profit	$129,000
Selling, general and administrative (including depreciation)	(67,000)
Operating Income	$62,000
Interest expense	(8,000)
Earnings before income taxes	$54,000
Income tax expense (50%)	(27,000)
Net earnings	$27,000

Marooth Corporation
Statement of Financial Position
On December 31

$ millions	1996	1995
Cash	$ $20,000	$ 6,000
Accounts receivable	40,000	60,000
Inventory	120,000	80,000
Total current assets	$180,000	$146,000
Property, Plant and Equipment	200,000	207,000
Total assets	$380,000	$353,000
Accounts payable	$40,000	$30,000
Notes payable	40,000	30,000
Total current liabilities	80,000	60,000
5% Mortgage payable	160,000	162,000
Total liabilities	$240,000	$222,000
Common stock, (30,000 shares)	120,000	120,000
Retained earnings	20,000	11,000
Stockholders' equity	$140,000	$131,000
Total liabilities and stockholders' equity	$380,000	$353,000

Required:

Compute the following ratios for the Marooth Company for the year ending December 31, 1996:

a. Profit margin ratio

b. Total assets turnover

c. Rate of return on total assets

d. Rate of return on common shareholders' equity

e. Earnings per share

f. Inventory turnover

g.   Current ratio

h.   Quick ratio

i.   Accounts receivable turnover

j.   Debt-equity ratio

k.   Interest coverage ratio

SOLUTIONS

1. ANALYSIS OF FINANCIAL STATEMENTS:

Marooth Corporation:

a. Profit margin ratio = 9.4% = $\dfrac{27,000 + (8,000 \times .50)}{329,000}$

b: Total assets turnover = .898 = $\dfrac{329,000}{(380,000 + 353,000)/2}$

c. Rate of return on total assets = 8.5% = $\dfrac{27,000 + (8,000 \times .50)}{(380,000 + 353,000)/2}$

    or   9.4% x .898

d. Rate of return on common shareholders' equity

  = 19.9% = $\dfrac{27,000}{(140,000 + 131,000)/2}$

e. Earnings per share = $.90 = $\dfrac{27,000}{30,000}$

f. Inventory turnover = 2 times = $\dfrac{200,000}{(120,000+80,000)/2}$

g. Current ratio = 2.25 to 1= $\dfrac{20,000+40,000+120,000}{80,000}$

h. Quick ratio = 0.75 to 1 = $\dfrac{20,000+40,000}{80,000}$

i. Accounts receivable turnover = 6.58 times = $\dfrac{329,000}{(40,000+60,000)/2}$

j. Debt-equity ratio = .632 to 1= $\dfrac{80,000 + 160,000}{380,000}$

j. Interest coverage ratio = 7.75 times = $\dfrac{54,000 + 8,000}{8,000}$

STUDY PLAN

1. Review the learning objectives, key terms, and exhibits for this chapter.

2. Financial statement analysis requires practice. Do as many Exercises in the text that you are able. Remember, in analyzing financial statements, you must know the industry as well as the company. Try to develop expectations of what you think the various ratios should be based on economic, industry, and firm information. A really interesting problem is Problem 30. In this problem you are a detective looking at 13 companies' financial information in common size analysis form. Based solely on the relationships presented, you are to identify the industries represented.

3. There are templates for Problems 17-14, 17-16, 17-18 and 17-34.